the natural snack
COOKBOOK

the natural snack
COOKBOOK

*151 good things
to eat*

by Jill Pinkwater

Four Winds Press   New York

LIBRARY OF CONGRESS CATALOGING IN PUBLICATION DATA

Pinkwater, Jill.
    The natural snack cookbook.

    Bibliography: p.
    SUMMARY: An introduction to healthful foods with recipes for
cakes, breads, sandwiches, puddings, and candies made with
natural ingredients.
    1. Snack foods—Juvenile literature.   2.   Food, Natural—Ju-
venile literature. [1. Cookery. 2. Food, Natural] I. Title.
TX740.P518   641.8   75–11717
ISBN 0–590–07374–5

PUBLISHED BY FOUR WINDS PRESS
A DIVISION OF SCHOLASTIC MAGAZINES, INC., NEW YORK, N.Y.
COPYRIGHT © 1975 BY JILL PINKWATER
ALL RIGHTS RESERVED
PRINTED IN THE UNITED STATES OF AMERICA
LIBRARY OF CONGRESS CATALOG CARD NUMBER: 75–11717
2 3 4 5   79 78 77 76

For Grandma Shapiro and Manus

Contents

the natural snack
COOKBOOK

1

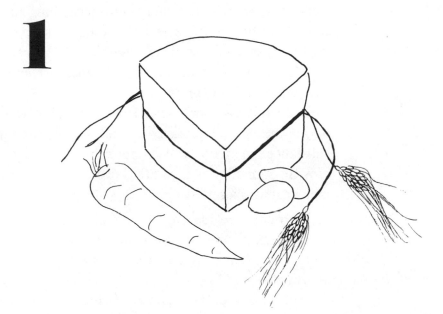

Healthful Foods: An Introduction

Everyone likes to eat between meals. We snack on cookies, candy, hotdogs, soda, cupcakes, cake, pizza, hamburgers, and ice cream. Sometimes it seems as if our mouths are always chewing on something; however, few of us stop to think whether or not the food we stuff into our mouths between meals is healthy. In fact, people joke that food which is good for them must taste bad.

This, of course, is nonsense. Healthful foods can be delicious and satisfying. What is not nonsense is the saying that "you are what you eat." Everything you eat influences your body in a positive or negative way. The food you eat will have a direct effect on your skin, hair, teeth, weight, and every cell in your body; in fact it will effect your physical and mental health and well-being for your entire life.

In order to fully understand how food influences your body, it is necessary for you to know something about nutrition. Nutrition is the science of food and its relation to health. It is a science which examines the materials (nutrients) found in food in order to discover exactly what they do for the human body.

The word nutrient comes from the Latin word *nutrire* which means "to nourish." A nutrient is, therefore, any substance in food which nourishes (feeds, promotes growth, supports) our bodies. Nutrients in food do three major services for us:

1. Nutrients provide energy or fuel (calories) needed by our bodies to maintain the proper body temperature and to carry out body activities (walking, running, swimming).
2. Nutrients are the materials which are necessary for growth, maintenance, and repair of our body tissues.
3. Nutrients are necessary for the regulation of body processes (digestion, breathing, circulation, and brain activity).

These nutrients are divided into six categories by scientists. We are all familiar with the names of these categories but we often do not quite understand just what they mean or just what they do for us. They are proteins, carbohydrates, fats, minerals, vitamins, and water. All nutrients work together to help your body function properly. The absence of only one or two will create an imbalance in your body and cause it to function poorly. For instance, an imbalance of nutrients might cause you to feel tired all of the time or it might cause your hair to get dull or your skin to break out in blemishes.

Proteins

Nutrients which are called proteins are essential to every cell in the body. They are necessary for the building, maintenance, and repair of *all* tissues including your hair which is mostly protein.

Proteins form hormones in your body (such as insulin, thyroxin, and adrenalin) and hormones regulate your body processes. This means that they control such important things as the rate of your heartbeat and breathing. Proteins also form antibodies (the disease- and infection-fighting mechanisms in your body) such as gamma globulin. They make hemoglobin, the red part of your blood which carries oxygen to all of the cells and carbon dioxide from all of the cells in your body. Proteins also supply energy to your body.

AMINO ACIDS   Proteins are combinations of between eighteen and twenty-two small elements called amino acids. Most amino acids can be made by your body but eight must be supplied by the food you eat. Since we all must get these eight amino acids from food in order for our bodies to form the proteins we need, they are called the *essential* (necessary) *amino acids.*

PROTEIN FOODS   There are two categories of protein foods. First there are the foods which supply all of the essential amino acids; these are called *complete protein foods.* Second there are foods which lack one or more essential amino acid; these are called *incomplete protein foods.*

COMPLETE PROTEIN FOODS

These are foods which are usually of animal origin such as meat, fish, poultry, eggs, milk and milk products (cheese, yoghurt, ice cream) , and gelatin.

Incomplete Protein Foods

These foods are incomplete in amino acids but are nevertheless good for us: cereals, whole grain flours, nuts, fruits, vegetables, and dried beans.

A balanced diet will include both kinds of protein foods. You can combine complete and incomplete protein foods to insure this balance by eating cereal with milk or whole grain bread with an egg or by having a snack of peanut butter on whole grain bread with a glass of milk or a container of yoghurt with some fruit.

Carbohydrates

Carbohydrates are nutrients which provide us with a good source of energy. If you include enough of them in your diet, your body will use less protein for energy and more protein for tissue building and repair. Carbohydrates also help your body to use fats in an efficient way.

There are many kinds of carbohydrates in food—starches, sugars, celluloses, dextrins, pectins, gums, and others. These carbohydrates usually supply your body with about half of its daily energy requirements. One kind of carbohydrate, cellulose, which is found in fruits, vegetables, and whole grain products, does not supply energy but supplies your body with bulk or "roughage." This roughage helps your intestines function properly.

Some of the foods which are rich in carbohydrates are cereals, whole grain products, milk, honey, fruit, vegetables, pastas, and sugar.

Fats

Fats provide another source of energy for your body. They also make up a part of many body cells and are, therefore, necessary to your body. Pound for pound and ounce for ounce, fats supply a bit more than twice as many calories as carbohydrates or proteins. Fats are divided into two groups—saturated fats (found in food of animal origin) and polyunsaturated fats (found in vegetable, grain, and nut oils).

Many fats (such as vegetable oils and butter) provide important amounts of vitamins. Polyunsaturated fatty acids which are found in vegetable and nut oils are essential to good health.

All fats are absorbed slowly by the body. This means that they keep you from feeling hungry for a long period of time. You can get your needed supply of daily fat in butter, margarine, cream, ice cream, whole milk, most cheese, vegetable and nut oils, meats, egg yolks, and nuts.

FATS AND OILY SKIN   Many people cannot tolerate too many fatty foods in their diets. Most people with oily skin problems (blemishes) are warned to stay away from foods rich in fats because it worsens their problems. If you are one of these people, stay away from food fried in oil, fatty meats, icings made with butter or margarine, and chocolate (which is 50 percent cocoa fat). You can get an ample supply of the fats and fatty acids needed by your body by drinking whole milk, eating some eggs, cheese, and whole grain baked products made with vegetable oils.

CHOLESTEROL AND FAT   Cholesterol is a fatlike substance which is made in the body; it is also supplied by foods of animal origin in the form of saturated fats. All body tissues, including the blood, have cholesterol in them. However, research has shown that too much cholesterol in the blood tends to lead to coronary heart disease. Fatty deposits build up in the inner walls of the blood vessels and hamper circulation.

Doctors usually advise people with a high cholesterol

level in their blood to reduce the amount of total saturated fats in their diets and to increase the amount of polyunsaturated fats. If you begin doing this when you are young, you will begin laying a foundation for a lifetime of good health. Some oils which can be used in cooking and baking and which will supply you with tasty sources of polyunsaturated fats are: corn, peanut, soybean, safflower, walnut, sesame, sunflower, olive, and corn germ oil. Some of these oils can be found in your local markets. The rest are available at health food stores.

Minerals

Minerals are nutrients which perform many jobs for your body. They are essential to your bones and teeth, are a necessary part of all cells and help regulate many vital body processes. In all, eighteen minerals are needed by your body but only a few of these have been studied enough to know much about them.

CALCIUM   Calcium is necessary for strong bones and teeth; in fact, 99 percent of the calcium in your body is in your bones and teeth. The other 1 percent is in your body fluids and tissues. Calcium aids in heart, nerve, and muscle function and helps your blood to clot (stop flowing when you are cut).

Calcium is found in large amounts in milk, milk products, dark-green leafy vegetables, dried peas and beans, seafood, sesame and sunflower seeds. It is found in lesser amounts in many other foods such as dried and fresh fruits, fruit juices, and nuts.

IRON   Your body needs less iron than calcium but the iron it needs is absolutely vital. It combines with protein to help copper make hemoglobin, the red, oxygen-carrying part of your blood.

Only a few foods have much iron in them: lean meats (especially liver, kidney, and heart), shellfish, dried peas and beans, dark-green leafy vegetables, dried fruits (including raisins), egg yolks, molasses, whole grain cereals and flours, nuts, pumpkin seeds, and sesame seeds. Many other foods have iron in them but in very small quantities.

IODINE Iodine is the mineral needed by your thyroid gland to make the hormone thyroxin. Thyroxin regulates many body functions including how fast your body uses up energy (calories). Too little iodine in your diet causes the thyroid gland (which is in your neck) to get very large. This condition, called a goiter, was once very common. However, today we get most of the iodine we need from iodized salt (salt which has iodine added to it) and the problem of goiters has practically disappeared.

We also get iodine from seafood and from any food grown in the iodine rich soils of our seacoasts.

MAGNESIUM AND PHOSPHORUS These minerals are found mostly in your bones and teeth. They help give strength to the hard parts of your body. Magnesium and phosphorus also help your body cells to use other nutrients properly. Magnesium is necessary for the nervous control of your muscles, and phosphorus helps the cells in your body absorb and transport other nutrients.

Magnesium is found in whole grain cereals and flours, nuts, dried fruits, dark-green leafy vegetables, liver, potatoes, and some seafoods.

Phosphorus is found in nuts, meats, fish, eggs, milk, milk products, dried peas and beans, yeast, sunflower seeds, and pumpkin. If you are getting enough protein and calcium in your diet, you are probably also getting enough phosphorus because they occur in many of the same foods.

Vitamins

Vitamins are nutrients which are needed by your body in very small amounts. Scientists have identified more than twelve major vitamins and have found that each vitamin has a specific, important function.

Vitamins are dissolved in your body either by water or by fats. Those soluble in fat are vitamins A, D, E, and K; those soluble in water are vitamin C and the B vitamins.

A *Warning*: A well-planned diet gives you all of the vitamins your body needs. Vitamin pills are unnecessary for people eating a good variety of healthy foods. The only times most people need vitamin pills are during infancy, pregnancy, and during certain illnesses. Don't prescribe for yourself. Some vitamins can be dangerous and will act as a poison in your system when taken in large quantities in pill form.

Vitamins	Function	Food
A	Needed for growth, normal night vision, and for keeping your skin, eyes, and inner body linings resistant to infection.	Found only in food of animal origin such as meat, fish, eggs, butter, whole milk, and whole milk cheese
Carotene	This is a substance which is changed into vitamin A in your body. An overdose of vitamin A in pill form can be very dangerous for you.	Dark-green leafy vegetables, deep yellow fruits (peaches, pumpkin, apricots), carrots, sweet potatoes, cherries, tomatoes, and peanuts
B B₁ (Thiamin) B₂ (Riboflavin) Niacin	These three vitamins are needed for the release of energy from foods, for growth, good appetite, digestion, healthy nerves, healthy	Meats, whole grain products, dried peas and beans, fresh vegetables, nuts, and milk

Vitamins	Function	Food
	skin, and good vision. Your body can make niacin from the essential amino acid called tryptophan. Therefore, a protein rich diet will also supply your niacin need.	
Folacin (folic acid) B_6 (pyridoxine) B_{12} (cobalamin)	These B vitamins are essential for the formation of your red blood cells. All three are needed by your body to process proteins, carbohydrates and fats; they are also needed for growth and for healthy nerve tissues.	Folacin and B_6: organ meats, poultry, fish, whole grains, peanuts, and most fruits and vegetables B_{12}: found only in foods of animal origin

There are at least five other vitamins and vitaminlike substances in the B group. However, although we know that they are essential nutrients, we do not have information regarding their exact functions in the body. For your general information, we will list them here: biotin, pantothenic acid, choline, inositol and para-amino benzoic acid. All of these B vitamins are found in a wide variety of foods but not much is known as yet regarding how much of each your body needs.

C	Vitamin C (ascorbic acid) is needed to help form and maintain the materials which hold your body cells together. It strengthens the walls of blood vessels and helps in the formation of your bones and teeth. It also aids in the healing of wounds and the fighting of infection.	Citrus fruits, dark-green leafy vegetables, strawberries, potatoes with their skins on, pineapple, cantaloupe, and papaya

Vitamins	Function	Food
D	Vitamin D helps your body use the calcium and phosphorus in foods. It also is necessary for the formation of strong bones and teeth. Overuse of vitamin D pills over a period of time can be very harmful to your body.	The main source of vitamin D is the action sunlight has on your skin. Only a few foods contain vitamin D naturally. They are egg yolk, liver, and fish. Other foods have vitamin D added to them such as fresh, evaporated, and dried milk
E	The exact functions of vitamin E have not yet been determined but it is known to be necessary for your body.	Vegetable oils, green leafy vegetables, nuts, fish, poultry, whole grain products, wheat germ, and eggs
K	This vitamin is a necessary part of the blood-clotting mechanism in your body.	Vitamin K is made in your body and is found in fresh leafy green vegetables, egg yolk and some animal fats. It can be easily destroyed by freezing.

Water

Every living thing must have water in order to survive. In fact, two thirds of your body weight is water. You use up this water by expelling vapor in your breath, by perspiring, and through your intestinal tract and kidneys. One can live for a long time without food but no one can live more than a few days without water. This is why it is considered an essential nutrient.

Food Additives

Now that you are acquainted with some of the necessary substances in the food you eat, it is important for you to know a little about substances which are added to foods by food processors. A food additive is any substance which is added to a basic, natural food. An additive may change the taste, texture, appearance, nutritional value, or the 'life span' of a food. Some additives are healthy or just harmless, and some are potentially dangerous for you.

HEALTHY AND HARMLESS ADDITIVES   Often food processors add extra nutrients to food. The most common nutrients added are vitamins and minerals although you will find that some foods have extra fats and carbohydrates added to them. The unfortunate thing is that these food processors often add the extra nutrients (especially vitamins and minerals) after they have removed the natural nutrients from the food by their processing methods. For example, many breakfast cereals would not need added nutrients if the original flours and grains in them had been left whole. Nutrients are removed in refining, cooking, and packaging procedures which are designed for inexpensive, mass marketing, and not always for good nutrition. However, a new federal law will require manufacturers and food processors to return all nutrients lost in processing to the food. It also requires a reduction of sugar content in breakfast cereals and that all food which is nonnutritive be labeled as such. Shopping for healthful food will become easier in years to come.

Other additives which provide nutrition and also add flavor to food are natural spices (such as pepper, cloves, cinnamon, salt, chili powder) and flavorings (such as natural vanilla, lemon, and almond extracts). The addition of spices and extracts often helps keep food from spoiling.

Then we have natural additives which change the texture of or thicken food such as gelatin (an animal product rich in protein), agar (a sea weed product which acts like gelatin), yeast and certain starches, sugars and gums such as corn starch, pectin and gum arabic (the sap of an acacia tree).

The final category of harmless additives is vegetable food coloring. Vegetable dyes are distilled from plants and are used to color foods so that they are more appealing or unusual (such as green or red or blue cake icings).

HARMFUL OR DOUBTFUL ADDITIVES We are living in a society where fresh produce, meats, and baked goods must be transported over great distances and then must sit on the shelves of markets for long periods of time. Because of this, food processors have discovered chemicals which will preserve and extend the life and good looks of most of the packaged food we eat.

These chemicals are supposedly tested and then "approved for consumption" by the federal government. What this means is that the chemicals are generally recognized as safe. However, research is now being done and it has shown that even though a food may have a tiny, acceptable level of a chemical in it and that individual food is harmless, your body tends to retain and store the chemical. This means that over a period of time, your body will accumulate more chemicals than are considered safe. One research group has discovered that many chemical preservatives inhibit the growth of human cell tissues and may even destroy them.

In addition to preservatives, food processors add chemicals to food which change the color, taste, and texture. These chemicals do much the same job as various natural ingredients but are easy to mass produce and, therefore, less expensive to use. Several research groups at universities are now studying the effect these chemicals have on the human body. One group has discovered that chemical flavorings (such as artificial vanilla and chocolate flavoring) and chemical colorings often cause a condition called hyperkinesis in some children. These children are so hyperactive (overactive and nervous) that they are unable to learn in school and have difficulty getting along with people at home and in school. When they are kept from eating convenience foods (soft drinks, processed cereals, packaged snacks) which are filled with chemical flavorings and colorings, their hyperactivity lessens and often goes away completely.

The lesson to be learned here is that we do not as yet know enough about chemical additives in our food to call them safe. You can do your body a great favor by trying to buy foods without additives in them; begin relying on your own homemade snacks and try avoiding those chemical-filled, quick-cooking, and ready-to-eat foods.

Buy as many fresh fruits or vegetables as possible and wash them well before using them. Many fruits are sprayed with insecticides and with chemical preservatives before they are packed and shipped. It is not as difficult as it may seem to insure your own good health; it simply takes a little more care when shopping. Read all labels and pass by those foods which seem to be more chemical than natural.

THE SECRET OF READING LABELS   There is a law which states that all ingredients must be listed on every food package. The law also states that the ingredient used most must be listed first, the ingredient used second most must be listed second, and so forth until all ingredients are listed. If you begin reading these lists on cans, packages, and boxes of food, you will find some surprising things. For example, many breakfast cereals which claim to be healthy for you have sugar listed first. In fact, some of these cereals have sugar listed in several places; they will list sugar in one place, brown sugar in another, dextrose (grape sugar) in another, sucrose (beet, turnip, carrot, maple sugar) in another, and lactose, lactine, or galactine (milk sugars) in another. Added up, you will see that some of these cereals are 75 percent sugar. No matter how many kinds of vitamins and minerals have been added, these sugar products can't be very good for you—especially as the first meal of the day.

Beware of products which have been named to fool you. Some products have honey listed as part of their names but have little or no honey in them.

Once you begin reading labels on packaged food, you will begin to become an educated consumer. You will also probably want to do more of your own cooking—using fresh ingredients on which you can rely.

The Recipes in this Book

The recipes in this book have been designed so that you will be able to snack on healthy food that also tastes good. With the exception of an occasional teaspoon of baking powder or soda, there are no chemicals and very few chemically treated foods in any of the recipes. Whenever possible, it is suggested that you use fresh fruit or canned or frozen fruit which has not been chemically treated (read the labels), whole grain or unbleached flours, and cooking oils without preservatives in them (usually found in health food stores).

In reading the recipes, you will notice that two very common ingredients are not used in this book. They are sugar and chocolate.

HISTORY OF SUGAR For most of human history, most people in the world used honey as a sweetener. Up until about 1700, very little sugar was exported to Europe from the parts of the world where it was grown. It was extremely expensive ($2.50 per half pound in 1700) and was, therefore, used mostly by the royal families and the upper classes. As trade increased, the amount of sugar reaching the western part of the world increased and by 1800, England alone was importing over 300 million pounds of sugar a year. Naturally, the price of sugar decreased and more and more people began using it.

In 1801, a scientist discovered how to manufacture sugar from beets and all of Europe began to have two inexpensive sources of sugar. Sugar quickly replaced honey as a popular sweetener; the fact that it had been the sweetener of the upper classes made it very appealing to other people. By 1840, during the industrial era, new machines were invented for refining sugar and it became even easier to get. At the same time, people were leaving their farms and moving to cities to work in factories. This meant that fewer people were keeping their own bee hives so honey became scarce. By 1900, more new inventions for inexpensively manufacturing white sugar made sugar cheap enough for everybody to afford. Today, the annual worldwide production of white cane sugar is over 13 billion pounds.

The only real set-backs in sugar production came during the world wars when sugar was difficult to import. Honey had a brief comeback but it was short-lived. Honey, once the universal sweet, became a luxury and sugar, once the sweetener of royalty, became the sweetener of the masses.

IS SUGAR BAD FOR YOU? The interesting thing about white sugar is that it can't really be called a food. It provides energy for your body but it has absolutely no nutritional value.

White sugar, brown sugar, and molasses all come from

the sugar cane plant. The juice of the cane is boiled and the various parts of the juice settle in layers in the huge boiling vats. The bottom-most layer contains what is known as blackstrap molasses, the second layer is Barbados molasses, the third is medium or regular molasses, the fourth is light molasses and the top layer is the white sugar crystals. All of the vitamins and minerals of the sugar cane settle towards the lower layers of this syrup leaving the top layer, the white sugar, totally free of nutrition. Brown sugar is simply a mixture of white sugar crystals and molasses so it has some nutritional value.

Because most of the sweetness of the sugar cane rises to the top of this syrup, dark molasses is not very sweet at all. The lighter molasses is sweet and was used for many years along with the less expensive brown sugar and maple sugar by people in America who could not afford white sugar. Since molasses has a rather strong taste (the darker the color, the stronger the taste), it is used today to supplement other sweeteners (such as honey) in a number of baked breads, cakes, and puddings.

The problem with both brown and white sugar is that, in addition to having little or no nutritional value, it is harmful to you. It is a pure carbohydrate which burns up so quickly in your body that it gives you a quick surge of energy which rapidly fades away. Your body then feels the need for another "lift" and you get the craving for more sugar (in the form of a candy bar or a very sweet cupcake). People who do not get adequate nutrition, become addicted to sugar and sugar-filled foods (bottled sodas, ice cream, candy, jellys, and jams) because their bodies have to rely on sugar for energy rather than on other foods which contain slower burning energy sources as well as vitamins and minerals.

In addition, sugar is extremely harmful to teeth; it tends

to promote decay especially during the years when your body is growing. Refined sugar also promotes an imbalance in the body which was recognized as early as 1929. Dr. F. G. Banting, one of the discoverers of insulin (a substance produced by the pancreas which allows your body to burn up sugar properly), warned that the disease diabetes had increased in proportion to the use of cane sugar.

No one expects you to never again eat food with sugar in it. It is simply suggested that you begin trying out snacks which are sweetened with honey and begin cutting back on your use of sugar.

HONEY Honey is manufactured by honey bees from the nectars they gather from flowers. It is predigested by the bees so it is very easily absorbed into our systems. Honey has a number of interesting and useful qualities.

First of all, honey contains a number of vitamins and minerals. It also contains two simple, natural sugars—levulose and dextrose—to give you energy; in addition, it contains enzymes which help in your digestion of it and other foods. Honey is more readily digested by your system than either milk or fruit juices because the natural sugars in it are the kind which do not have to be processed by your body. They are absorbed directly, "as is."

Honey has a natural preservative quality which helps other food to last longer. For example, a cake baked with honey will stay fresh longer than one baked with sugar. Honey is also an amazing food because bacteria cannot survive in it. Many experiments have been performed where scientists have tried to grow the deadliest bacteria in honey without success. Honey has such a long life that honey found in sealed jars in Egyptian tombs (3300 years old) was found to be almost liquid; this 3300-year-old honey had also kept its delicate aroma.

Honey has been used for thousands of years to dress wounds—even in surgery. Today, doctors in England are again experimenting using honey as surgical dressings after major operations. They are finding that it prevents bacteria from invading the wounds and that it also promotes quick healing. Last of all, honey has also been used for thousands of years to dress burns and to cure digestive problems.

However, nicest of all for your cooking, honey comes in a wide variety of flavors and aromas. Some of these are wildflower, orange blossom, clover, avocado, blueberry, mangrove, lime tree, and peach blossom honey, to name a few. You can take your choice as to which honey you want to use and add the delicate flavor and smell of a favorite blossom to your cooking.

CHOCOLATE As stated before, there are no chocolate-flavored recipes in this book. The reasons for this are simple. Chocolate has a very concentrated, rich fat content which is not good for people with any kind of skin blemish problem. Also, most chocolate products are loaded with sugar. The exceptions are baking chocolate—which is chocolate in its pure form—and some unsweetened cocoa products. In addition, most cookbooks have many chocolate-flavored recipes in them. It might be nice for you to discover some of the other cooking flavors that are delicious, delicate, and satisfying.

However, for those of you who do not have skin problems and are, therefore, not worried about chocolate's 50 percent fat content, it is good to know that chocolate is a natural product which contains many vitamins and minerals. If you decide to cook and bake with chocolate, use only the unsweetened kind in its pure form (read the label on the package) and try to avoid all high sugar chocolate products.

There are recipes in this book which contain carob powder (sometimes called carob flour). Carob is another natural flavoring which tastes very much like chocolate. It has the benefit of being naturally sweet (chocolate is naturally bitter) and has a very low fat content. Most health food stores sell carob powder and if you do not want to forego the delicious taste of chocolate, but must avoid chocolate, try carob as a substitute. It, too, is rich in vitamins and minerals and will not cause your face to break out.

Note to Dieters

All food has calories. Food, as you've read so far, is used by your body to make energy, and to help form and maintain body cells. Some food, however, has more calories than other food and is used up more slowly by your body. Think about what it is like to build a fire. If you put a ten pound log on the fire, it will take a long time to burn. If you put ten pounds of paper on the fire, it will burn up very quickly. In the same way, one ounce of food with 100 calories (such as an ounce of licorice candy or one ounce of chocolate covered peppermints) will take a much longer time for your body to burn than one ounce of food with 10 calories (such as one ounce of fresh strawberries).

When your body does not burn up all of the food you eat to make energy or new cells, it turns the food into body fat. Your body makes three types of fat: the first type is used for padding—on your fingertips, on the palms of your hands, on the balls of your feet, on your toes, and on your buttocks. This padding is like having small cushions all over your body to protect it in places which get a great deal of use.

The second kind of fat is found all over your body. It is a thin layer of fat just under your skin. This fat acts like a warehouse for extra energy. Your body uses it when it can't get enough calories from the food you eat by turning this fat into energy. If ever you have to go for a long period of time without food, this fat will sustain your body. You might feel hungry but your body will continue to function.

The third type of fat is extra fat your body doesn't really need. It is made by your body when you are eating more calories than your body can use up in its various activities. When you diet, you are trying to get rid of this extra fat. The way to do this is to eat fewer calories and to exercise. Exercise helps your body to burn up calories faster. Your goal is, of course, to reach a point where you eat enough calories to give you energy and help you grow without allowing your body to make extra fat.

This is extremely tricky because no two people use up calories in exactly the same way. You probably have friends who can sit around eating pizza and ice cream and not gain an ounce. Think about how cars with large engines use gasoline very quickly and will travel only eight or ten miles on a gallon. Cars with small engines might be able to travel fifteen or twenty miles on a gallon of the same gasoline. You may have the kind of body that burns up calories fast but if you are overweight, you probably have a body which burns up calories slowly. In addition, you are simply eating too much or you are eating foods with too many calories (such as chocolate candy or cake or soda). The point is, don't compare yourself to your friends when judging how many calories or what kind of food to eat. With the help of your family doctor, you can discover just how much you need to eat in order to be healthy and to lose weight effectively.

Healthful food doesn't necessarily mean low calorie food. If you are trying to lose weight, stick to fruit snacks. If you stick to your diet program now, you will be able to enjoy the other snacks in this book later on. If you can't resist trying a recipe or two, then taste only a small portion of it and give the rest away. Remember—even fruit has calories and if you eat enough of it, you will have trouble losing weight.

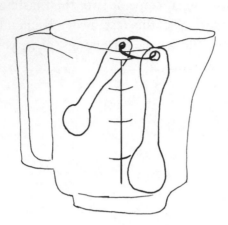

Cooking Terms and Measurements

When I was a child, I remember standing in the kitchen watching my grandmother cook. She never measured ingredients in the established way; grandma put in a pinch of this, a glass or a handful of that and then tasted. Grandma told me that her mother and grandmother had cooked in the same way and began teaching me.

However, I wanted to copy down her recipes. In order to record them accurately, I began to measure her handfuls, glasses and pinches in standard measuring cups and spoons. Today I am glad I did because it's been many years since I put those recipes on paper and it would be difficult to remember exactly what size handfuls and glasses my grandmother used.

All recipes are written with the same cooking terms and

the same measurements so that they can be passed from person to person, from generation to generation and even from country to country accurately. This chapter will describe and explain the.standard cooking measurements and cooking terms you will need to make the recipes in this and other cookbooks.

Measurements

MEASURING SPOONS   Measuring spoons usually come in sets of four. Each set includes one tablespoon, one teaspoon, ½ teaspoon and ¼ teaspoon. There are several simple rules you must know regarding measuring spoons.

1. *Never* use flatware teaspoons or tablespoons to measure ingredients. *Always* use the standard measuring spoons.
2. *Always* measure out *level* spoonfuls of ingredients unless told otherwise (see rule 3) . This is done in the following way:
   a. Put the ingredient (spice, margarine, baking soda) into the spoon.
   b. Take the back, level side of a table knife and rest it on the edge of the measuring spoon near the handle.
   c. Gently move the knife to the tip of the spoon, scraping the excess ingredient away. This is only necessary for powdered and solid ingredients.
3. The exception to rule 2 is when a recipe says to use a heaping spoonful of an ingredient.

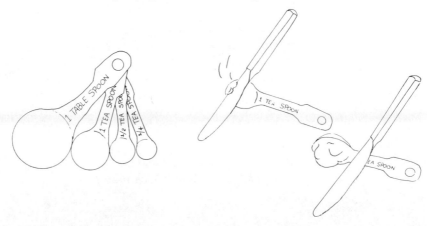

MEASURING CUPS   There are two types of measuring cups available in stores. First there are single cup measures. These are transparent glass or plastic cups which are marked to indicate fractions of a cupful (for example: ½ cup, ¼ cup) as well as liquid ounces. These cups come in either a one cup, two cup, or even a three cup size.

The second type of measuring cup is really a set of cups similar to the set of measuring spoons. Each set usually includes a cup, ½ cup, ⅓ cup and ¼ cup measure.

Each type of measuring cup has its advantage. The transparent, large cups will allow you to measure liquid ounces as well as fractions of cupsful. The set of cups allows you to measure ingredients without rinsing and drying the cup between each operation. For example, if you need ¼ cup of honey and 1 cup of flour, you simply use different cups. The drawback of the measuring cup sets is that they don't indicate liquid ounces.

The best way to cook is to have both kinds of cups but this is not absolutely necessary. Learning to use one type of measuring cup accurately is all you need to do.

Cooking Terms and Measurements

LEVEL CUPSFUL   Try to measure your ingredients in level cupsful. Do this in the following way:

LIQUIDS:

Always set the cup down on an even surface. Don't try to hold it in the air to read the measurement. This is especially important with liquids because they will slosh around if you try to hold the cup at eye level and you will not get an even measure.

DRY INGREDIENTS:

1. In the measuring cup sets, use the back of a knife to even off the measure (as you did with the measuring spoons) .
2. In a large, transparent measuring cup, gently spread the ingredient so that it is even.
3. *Never* press or pat dry ingredients down to make an even measure. Ingredients such as flour compress easily and you'll be using more than you need if you do this. The exception to this rule is brown sugar. To measure it correctly, you must pack it into the cup.

BUTTER OR MARGARINE:

1. Soften the butter or margarine by keeping it out of the refrigerator for about a half hour.
2. Press the butter or margarine into the cup firmly until the cup is as full as the recipe calls for.
3. If you are using a set of cups, level the butter or margarine off with the back of a knife.
4. If you are using a large cup measure and need only perhaps ½ cupful, gently press the butter or margarine down into the cup with the back of a spoon and make it as level as possible.

OR

Modern packaging has made it easy for us to measure butter or margarine without using measuring cups. Most brands of butter and margarine come in one-pound packages which are divided into ¼ pound sticks. Some of these sticks of butter and margarine have markings on their paper wrappers which indicate tablespoon and cup measures. If they don't, use the following table:

¼ stick of margarine or butter (¹⁄₁₆ pound) = ⅛ cup
½ stick of margarine or butter (⅛ pound) = ¼ cup
1 stick of margarine or butter (¼ pound) = ½ cup
2 sticks of margarine or butter (½ pound) = 1 cup
3 sticks of margarine or butter (¾ pound) = 1½ cups
4 sticks of margarine or butter (1 pound) = 2 cups

ABBREVIATIONS Most cookbooks abbreviate standard terms in order to save space. The following are the most common of these abbreviations.

teaspoon	= tsp. or t.	pounds	= lbs.
tablespoon	= tbs. or T.	pint	= pt.
cup	= C.	quart	= qt.
ounce	= oz.	gallon	= gal.
pound	= lb.		

LIQUID (FLUID) OUNCES VS WEIGHT OUNCES There are two kinds of ounces you must know about in order to buy ingredients and to cook. The first kind of ounce is a weight measure (for example, 16 ounces in 1 pound). The second kind of ounce is a liquid or fluid ounce (for example, 8 ounces in 1 cup).

One cup of feathers (8 liquid ounces) and one cup of pebbles (8 liquid ounces) will not weigh the same. This is important to remember because some canned and packaged products are labeled in liquid ounces and some in

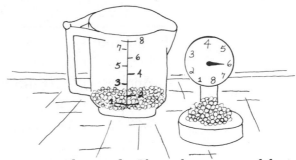

weight ounces and pounds. If you buy a can of fruit to use in a recipe that requires ¾ of a cup (6 fluid ounces) and the can is labeled "net weight 6 ounces," you may find that the fruit does not fill up the cup to the ¾ measure.

Most cooking instructions concern themselves with liquid ounces. Therefore, when you are buying ingredients, either choose those labeled in liquid ounces or learn to estimate what you need. The following list will help you to estimate equivalents.

EQUIVALENTS:

Eggs:	4 to 7 whole eggs	= 1 cup of eggs
	8 to 12 egg whites	= 1 cup of egg whites
	1 egg yolk	= 1 tbs. egg yolk
Flour:	1 lb. unbleached	= approximately 3¾ cups
	1 lb. whole wheat	= 3½ cups
Honey:	1 lb. honey	= approximately 1⅓ cups
Yeast:	1 cake yeast	= 1 tbs. active dry yeast
Gelatin:	1 tbs. gelatin	= 1 small envelope of gelatin
Cream:	1 cup heavy cream	= 2 cups whipped cream

Dried Fruit:

Raisins:	1 lb.	= 2¾ cups
Apricots:	1 lb.	= 3 cups
Dates:	1 lb.	= 2¼ cups
Pears:	1 lb.	= 2⅔ cups
Prunes:	1 lb. pitted	= 2½ cups

Fresh Fruit:
  Bananas: 1 lb. (3 to 4 medium) = 2 cups mashed
  Apples: 1 lb. (3 medium)   = 3 cups sliced
  Berries: 1 pint   = 2 cups
  Lemon: 1 medium   = 3 tbs. juice
                                         2 tsp. grated rind
  Orange: 1 medium   = 6–8 tbs. juice
                                         2–3 tbs. grated rind

Nuts:
  Almonds: 6 oz. whole shelled = 1 cup
                1 lb. ground   = 2⅔ cups
                1 lb. slivered   = 5⅔ cups
  Coconut: 3½ oz. grated   = 1 cup
  Peanuts: 1 lb. shelled   = 2¼ cups
  Pecans: 1 lb. shelled   = 4 cups
  Walnuts: 1 lb. chopped   = 1 cup
                1 lb. in shell   = 2½ cups shelled

You measure liquid or fluid ounces by using the ounce lines on your transparent measuring cup. If you do not have such a cup, use the following table:

1 liquid oz. = 2 tbs. or ⅛ cup
2 liquid oz. = 4 tbs. or ¼ cup
3 liquid oz. = 6 tbs.
4 liquid oz. = 8 tbs. or ½ cup
5 liquid oz. = 10 tbs.
6 liquid oz. = 12 tbs. or ¾ cup
7 liquid oz. = 14 tbs.
8 liquid oz. = 16 tbs. or 1 cup

Finally, here are some miscellaneous measurements which will be useful to you:

3 teaspoons   = 1 tablespoon
4 tablespoons   = ¼ cup

5⅓ tablespoons	= ⅓ cup
1 cup	= ½ pint
2 cups	= 1 pint
4 cups	= 1 quart
2 pints	= 1 quart
4 quarts	= 1 gallon

Cooking Terms

ABSORBENT PAPER: Any paper which will easily absorb moisture. This is used to drain greasy or wet food. It can be paper towels, paper napkins, a clean brown paper bag, or brown wrapping paper.

BAKE: To cook in the oven.

BASTE: To spoon or brush liquid (usually butter, margarine, honey, or natural juices) over the food as it cooks. Basting keeps the food moist and adds flavor to it. With certain baked foods, basting gives the food a shiny glaze.

BEAT: The *vigorous* mixing of an ingredient or ingredients with a spoon, fork, egg beater, or electric mixer.

BEAT-IN: To beat in is to add one ingredient to another while beating.

BLANCHED: A term usually used for nuts. A food which has had boiling water poured over it to loosen its skin has been blanched. A blanched nut is therefore a nut minus its dark skin.

BLEND: To thoroughly mix together ingredients. The recipes will tell you when this means to blend in an electric blender. However, electric blending really means to puree something and puree is to make a food into a smooth paste.

BOIL: To cook a liquid until bubbles are rising to the surface very rapidly.

BROIL: To cook a food directly over or under the heat so that the food is exposed to the heating source. You can broil in the broiler of your oven, over a wood or charcoal fire, or in one of the many portable broilers which are being made today.

BROWN: To cook in a little bit of oil or fat until the food is lightly brown.

BRUSH: Using a pastry brush, your finger, or a spoon, you brush the surface of a food with a liquid (honey, oil, melted butter, or margarine) .

CHOP: To cut ingredients into very small pieces.

CELLOPHANE WRAP: A thin, pliable, transparent paper sold in rolls in markets and in grocery stores for wrapping food.

CORE: To remove the center portion (seeds and stem) of a fruit.

CREAM: Thoroughly smoothing ingredients with a heavy spoon. For example, creaming margarine or butter and honey together in baking. The best way to do this is to have the margarine or butter at room temperature before you begin. If you use liquid vegetable oil instead of a solid fat, you won't have to cream; you'll simply have to stir the ingredients.

CUBE: To cut into small, cubelike pieces.

CUT-IN: Using two table knives, you cut butter or margarine into flour. This is used in pastry making.

DASH: A dash of a spice or of salt is less than ⅛ teaspoon. You add a dash to other ingredients by shaking the saltcellar or spice container once or twice over the ingredients. Be sure when you do this with spices that there is a lid with tiny holes on the container.

DICE: To cut an ingredient into very, very tiny cubes.

DOT: To place small lumps of an ingredient (usually margarine or butter) on another ingredient before cooking.

DUST: This is the covering of a food or a baking tool with a very light layer of a dry ingredient such as flour.

FOLD-IN: When you fold in ingredients, you gently fold one ingredient over the other with a large spoon. Starting from the side of the bowl farthest from you, move the spoon down to the bottom of the bowl. Bring it along the bottom of the bowl toward you and then up your side of the bowl. You then bring the mixture over the center of the bowl. You keep doing this until the mixture is pretty well mixed.

GARNISH: To decorate a finished product with nuts, fruit, parsley, olives, and so on.

GRATE: To rub a food on a grater, cutting it into tiny bits.

GREASE: To rub a solid shortening (usually butter or margarine) over the inside of a baking pan, loaf pan, casserole dish, or cookie sheet.

GRILL: The same as broil.

GRIND: You grind food by putting it through a grinder which cuts it into very tiny bits. There are both hand and electric grinders on the market. Fortunately, you can now buy many foods which have been ground for you such as ground nuts. Some foods can be ground in a mortar and pestle (such as pepper and other spices) or in an electric blender (such as nuts).

ICE: To spread icing or frosting on a cake or cupcake.

KNEAD: To mix and roll thoroughly with your hands (see bread making chapter for detailed instructions, p. 132).

MINCE: To chop a food into very, very tiny irregular-shaped pieces.

OIL: To rub a liquid cooking oil over the inside of a baking pan, loaf pan, casserole dish or cookie sheet.

PAN BROIL: To cook in a skillet or frying pan with little or no oil or fat.

PARE: Peeling off the skin of a fruit or vegetable.

PINCH: A tiny amount of an ingredient (usually salt or a spice). You measure it by picking up a bit of the ingredient between your thumb and your first finger.

PUNCH DOWN: A term used in bread and roll making. It means to force the air out of a yeast dough that has risen by using your fist. You do not have to use a great deal of force.

ROLL OUT DOUGH: Using a rolling pin which has been rubbed with flour to press down and shape dough (see pie chapter for details, p. 221).

SCALD: To heat a liquid just to the boiling point without letting it boil or to plunge a solid food into boiling water for a minute.

SEPARATE: To separate eggs is to separate the yolk from the white. This is done while the uncooked egg is cold. Crack open the egg over a small dish and pour the egg yolk from one half of the shell to the other. The egg white will drip into the dish. You can also use a small tea strainer for the job. Place the strainer over a small cup or dish. Carefully break the egg and pour it into the strainer without breaking the yolk. The white will drain through the strainer into the cup or dish (see illustration).

SHELLED: A nut or vegetable (such as peas) *without* its shell.

SHORTENING: Any fat or oil used in cooking.

SHRED: To cut or tear an ingredient into thin slivers.

SIFT: To shake dry ingredients through a flour sifter or sieve.

SIMMER: Cooking a liquid or ingredients in a liquid gently below the boiling point. The liquid should just barely be moving with an occasional bubble rising to the surface.

SLIVER: When you slice food into long, thin pieces, you get

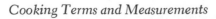

slivers. Some foods, such as nuts, can now be bought already slivered.

STEAM: Cooking over boiling water in a tightly covered pot. The food is not put directly in the water but is placed above it on a rack or on a plate which is resting on a perforated tin can (see illustration). The steam from the boiling water cooks the food.

STIFF BUT NOT DRY: When you are beating egg whites and the recipe says "beat until stiff but not dry," you beat the egg whites until they stand in peaks when you lift your beater out of the bowl. They should look shiny and moist.

STIR: When you stir, you blend your ingredients with a spoon by using wide, circular movements. Stirring is less vigorous than beating.

WAXED PAPER: Waxed paper is a specially coated paper sold in rolls in markets. It is extremely useful in many baking procedures.

WHIP: When you whip an ingredient (usually icings, frostings, and whipped cream), you beat it with an egg beater, a fork, a wire whisk, or an electric mixer until it is fluffy and puffy.

3

Tools You'll Need

People often think that in order to be a good cook, they must go out and buy all sorts of fancy tools and pots and pans. This is not true. Of course it is nice to own beautiful, matching pots, pans, and baking dishes; it even helps, for an occasional special recipe, to have a special fancy pot or pan but these luxuries are not necessary. The one rule you must remember about cooking equipment is to always make sure that it is as spotless as possible. This is especially important for any pan, tin, or dish you are going to bake in. Remove all old spots and burned in char before using them. If you do this, your baked products will cook more evenly, they will not have the added flavor of some past cooking, and they will be less likely to stick to the pan.

Each recipe in this book will tell you what tools you will need in order to make it. The following is a list of general cooking equipment that most people have in their kitchens. If you don't have a certain item, the list will, when possible, give you suggestions for a substitute item.

Forks

One regular kitchen fork: Used for testing doneness, mashing certain foods, beating some foods, and making air holes in the top of pies.

Knives

One large, sharp cutting knife: Used to cut fruits, chop up nuts and other foods, trim the edges of pies, and so forth.

One paring knife: This is a small, sharp knife used for peeling fruit and for coring fruit. It can also be used for cutting around the edge of grapefruit so that the pieces can come out easily if you don't have the following.

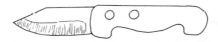

One grapefruit knife: A small, flexible knife with serrated edges (edges with tiny "teeth"). It is used for loosening grapefruit pieces from their skin.

Two regular table knives: For cutting in shortening in pastry dough, for leveling ingredients, and for other general use.

Spoons

One wooden spoon (or one very large metal spoon with a
long handle) : Used for mixing.

One kitchen tablespoon: Used for mixing smaller amounts
of food.

One kitchen teaspoon: Used for mixing even smaller
amounts of food and for tasting.

One set of measuring spoons: There is no substitute for
these. You must acquire a set.

Other Tools

Electric mixer: Used for beating batters, whipping cream,
and general mixing. You *do not* need an electric mixer
although they are helpful to have. You can substitute
a mixer with the following.

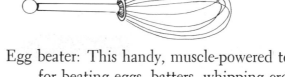

Egg beater: This handy, muscle-powered tool can be used
for beating eggs, batters, whipping cream, and so on.
It takes a little longer than an electric mixer but provides good exercise for you.

Wire whisk: This is a light metal tool used for beating lightweight ingredients such as eggs and cream. If you have
one, use it. If you don't have one, use one of the above
tools or a kitchen fork to do light beating.

Flour sifter or sieve: A flour sifter is a good kitchen tool to
have but it is not necessary. I have always used a
tightly woven sieve for sifting flour. A sieve can also
be used for washing off berries and vegetables and for
draining foods which have been presoaked or fried.

Spatula: Sometimes called a pancake or an egg flipper. Excellent for removing cookies from baking pans and for turning over certain pan-baked breads such as chappatis and tortillas. This is an essential tool which has no substitute.

Rubber scraper: This tool has a wooden or metal handle and a rubber end piece. It is handy for getting every last bit of a batter, icing, or custard mix out of the mixing bowl. It's nice to have but not essential.

Pastry brush: This is a small brush with a wire handle and soft, long bristles. You use it for brushing the top of breads, rolls, and other baked goods with butter, margarine, honey, or egg. If you don't have one, you can use a new, unused soft paint brush, your fingers, a spoon, or a piece of paper towel to do the job.

Potato masher: A tool used for mashing potatoes or other soft ingredients. A fork can be used as a substitute tool.

Mortar and pestle: The wooden bowl of this set of tools is called a mortar and the wooden crusher is the pestle. They are used together to crush spices, nuts, garlic, and any other ingredients that are small and need crushing.

Oven thermometer: If your oven does not have a good built-in thermometer (most older ovens don't), then it is important that you buy an oven thermometer. Most supermarkets or hardware stores sell them for under $2.00. A good oven thermometer will mean fewer burned or undercooked baked foods.

Tools You'll Need

Rolling pin: A must for pie crusts, crackers, and certain biscuits.

Biscuit and cookie cutters: Nice to have but you can also use the top of a drinking glass to cut round shapes or you can use one of the regular table knives and cut freeform shapes (stars, squares, diamonds).

Bread board or wooden work board: These are good for rolling out pie and cookie doughs and for kneading bread. They are also useful when you are cutting up various ingredients (they keep you from marking up the surface of a counter or table). However, you can also use a clean formica counter top or table or the top of a wooden kitchen table for rolling out dough. Just remember to clean and dry the counter or table top well before using it.

Cake rack: This is a metal rack used for cooling cakes, pies, cookies, breads, etc. Baked goods are placed on it so that air can freely circulate around them. Baked products tend to come out less soggy and more tasty when cooled on a rack. You can make your own cake rack by using a very clean rack from your oven or even one of those metal mesh pan covers used to prevent grease from spattering or even a steamer tray. Be sure to prop up the grease catcher or oven rack on several cups or cans so that it is steady (see illustration). And make sure that anything you use is absolutely clean. Cookies that taste like bacon grease are no treat.

Grater: Metal tools used to grate or shred ingredients. Hold the grater in one hand and rub the ingredient against it with the other hand.

Dishes, Bowls, and Cups

Mixing bowls of various sizes: Metal mixing bowls are best because they can be put into the freezer if necessary. However, glass mixing bowls are fine. You do not need a matched set of blowls. Just make sure that you have at least one very large bowl and several smaller bowls.

One set of measuring cups (or one large transparent measuring cup): There is no substitute for a proper measuring cup so if you don't have one, you must buy one.

Some small bowls and dishes: Several small bowls and saucers will be needed for soaking ingredients (such as raisins and yeast) or setting aside measured ingredients for use as you cook.

Pots and Pans

One medium saucepan, one large saucepan, one small saucepan: All three of these will be needed for cooking certain custards, applesauce, fruit concoctions, and for melting butter or margarine.

One glass baking pan: Good for baked puddings and custards if you do not have custard cups (see chapter on custards, p. 81).

Heavy, large frying pan (or large griddle): Needed for pan-baked desserts, breads, and crackers.

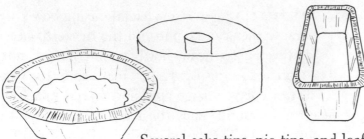

Several cake tins, pie tins, and loaf pans: These can all be
bought in reusable tinfoil for very little money in supermarkets if you don't have them in your home.

Cookie sheet: If you don't have a cookie sheet, do what I
do. I bake my cookies in large, glass baking pans.

Muffin tins: If you are going to make muffins or cupcakes,
you absolutely need muffin tins. There is no substitute.

Double boiler: Two pots with a cover. One pot fits inside
of the other. Water is placed in the bottom pot and
the food is placed in the top pot. The food is cooked
gently by the heat coming from the boiling water. You
will need one of these for some of the recipes. It is
difficult to make an adequate substitute.

Once again, use your imagination and substitute one tool
for another if you can. It's nice to have fancy equipment
such as a blender, electric mixer, nut chopper, and food
grinder but you can do without them. After all, people have
been cooking without these things for most of human
history.

Tools You'll Need   *40*

4

Beverages

Beverages are often the most difficult problem to solve for a person who has decided to eat healthy food. There are so many canned and bottled sodas and sweet drinks available that it is difficult to avoid them. Everyone likes to have a cool, refreshing drink occasionally—and some people, especially during the warm summer months or after strenuous activity, need a number of glasses of cold liquid a day.

Unfortunately, with the exception of dietetic drinks that are loaded with chemicals, all flavored sodas and most fruit drinks available are full of sugar. However, there is a way to avoid these chemical and sugar-packed drinks and that is to begin reading labels on cans and bottles. In addition, this section will give you some ideas about how to make your own carbonated drinks using fruit juices for flavoring.

There will also be some ideas for thick, tasty drinks that are practically meals—great for breakfasts and snacks that will fill you up for an entire afternoon.

But first let us examine the kinds of statements you will find on labels of fruit drinks so that you will know what to look for and how to make a choice. All of these fruit drinks can be found canned, bottled, in waxed containers, or frozen.

Juice: Juice is the strained liquid from a fruit or vegetable (carrot or lemon juice). After using, refrigerate the leftover juice with the container *covered* or it will lose flavor and vitamins.

Fruit Juice Drink: This is usually a drink made of 50 percent fruit juice and 50 percent water and sweeteners (usually sugar).

Fruit Drink: This is another mixture of juice, water, and sweetener but any fruit drink can have as little as 10 percent juice in it.

Nectar: This is the richest fruit drink available. It includes the juice of the fruit and most of the pulped fruit. Nectars are thicker than juices and can be used in lesser quantity when making drinks. They are good as they are or, if you like thinner drinks, diluted a bit with some water. Most supermarkets have some nectars on the shelves but many of them have sugar added unnecessarily. The widest assortment of pure nectars can be found in health food stores.

Concentrates: These are juices that have been condensed down to four times their original strength. You can find them in cans on the shelves or in the frozen food areas of markets. In health food stores you can buy concentrates such as apple and cherry in bottles. These can be used for sweetening baked products as well as for making drinks. A good formula for making a drink with a concentrate is three portions of water (or carbonated water) to one part concentrate.

Orange Juice Products: The federal government's Food and Drug Administration has made your job a little easier when you are shopping for orange juice products. In September 1972, a law was passed requiring that all orange juice products be accurately labeled. Each drink containing orange juice must state the percentage of juice in it. Perhaps the law will extend to all fruit drinks some day.

In the meantime, read labels. Try to buy juices, nectars, or concentrate with no sugar or chemicals added. Watch out because many juices and concentrates state in large letters that they are 100 percent pure juice and then in small letters say "sweetened" or "with sugar added."

Above all, after reading and trying out the recipes in this section, don't ignore the delicious taste of a glass of plain, ice cold milk, apple juice, pineapple juice, grape juice, or whatever your favorite natural drink happens to be.

Carbonated Sodas

It is really simple to make your own carbonated sodas. The formula below will allow you to choose your favorite fruit juice and make a soda out of it. With the aid of a little bit of honey, you can make these drinks as sweet as you like.

1 serving

INGREDIENTS

1 large bottle of carbonated water (also called seltzer or soda water)

unsweetened fruit juice

honey

ice

EQUIPMENT

1 drinking glass

1 tableware teaspoon

---

1. Fill your glass about halfway full of juice.
2. Add some carbonated water and stir. Taste.
3. If you want your drink sweeter, add some honey and stir.
4. If you want your drink richer or stronger in flavor, add some more juice and stir.
5. If you want your drink lighter, add some more carbonated water and stir.
6. Add ice cubes if you wish, and drink.

You will rapidly become an expert at mixing sodas to your liking. Instead of serving bottled drinks at your next party or gathering of friends, try serving the ingredients for homemade carbonated sodas and let everyone mix their own.

Mulled Cider or Apple Juice

On a cold winter or fall day, mulled cider or apple juice seems to travel instantly to one's bones in a warm glow. Try this hot drink the next time you are feeling chilled. **4 servings**

INGREDIENTS	EQUIPMENT
4 cups apple juice or apple cider, unsweetened	1 large saucepan
	1 tableware teaspoon
4 cinnamon sticks	measuring cup
3 whole cloves	
nutmeg	

1. Put the apple cider or juice, the cinnamon sticks, and the cloves into the saucepan.
2. Sprinkle a dash of nutmeg on the top of the cider or juice.
3. Heat over a low flame until it is simmering. Simmer for 5 minutes. Remove cloves.
4. Serve in mugs or cups with one cinnamon stick in each.

Frosteds

Frosteds are drinks made with ice cream. You need a blender to make them in most cases. If you have patience and a strong arm, you can do without a blender.   **1 serving**

Directions: To make a frosted, you place all of the ingredients in the blender, cover it and blend for about 10 seconds on high speed. Drink it immediately.

To make a frosted without a blender, you put your ice cream in a large bowl, soften it with a heavy spoon, add the rest of your ingredients and beat vigorously with an electric mixer or egg beater. Drink it immediately.

VARIATIONS BANANA FROSTED

1 cup milk

1 large scoop of ice cream

1 banana, sliced (for hand beating, use a ripe banana and mash it very well)

APRICOT FROSTED	PEACH FROSTED
½ cup apricot nectar	½ cup peach nectar
½ cup milk	½ cup milk
1 scoop of vanilla ice cream	1 scoop vanilla ice cream

Lemon Milk Drink

1 serving

INGREDIENTS

2 tbs. lemon juice
1 tbs. honey
1 cup milk

EQUIPMENT

egg beater or electric mixer
1 large bowl
measuring cup
measuring spoon

1. Pour all ingredients into the mixing bowl.
2. Beat the mixture until it is fluffy.
3. Taste to see if you want more honey. If so, add some and beat again.
4. Pour into glasses and drink.

Orange Milk Drink

If you like the way milk sherbet tastes, you'll like this and the following drink.

1 serving

INGREDIENTS

½ cup orange juice
¾ cup ice cold milk

EQUIPMENT

egg beater or electric mixer
1 large bowl
measuring cup

1. Pour the juice and the milk into a bowl.
2. Beat the milk/juice mixture until it is fluffy.
3. Pour into glasses and drink.

Orange Drink for a Small Crowd

This recipe makes about one quart of delicious orange drink. Make it about a half hour before serving because it must chill for a while.

4 servings

INGREDIENTS	EQUIPMENT
3 cups water	1 very large mixing bowl
1 6 oz. can frozen, concentrated, unsweetened orange juice	1 large spoon for mixing
	measuring cup
1 cup instant nonfat dry milk	soup ladle
nutmeg	

1. Place all of the ingredients in the large mixing bowl.
2. Mix vigorously with a spoon until the juice has dissolved and all of the ingredients are well blended.
3. Chill in the refrigerator for 30 minutes.
4. Serve in the bowl with a little nutmeg sprinkled on top of the drink.
5. Let each person fill their own glass with the aid of a soup ladle.

Berry Shake

You need a blender for this drink. It's one of the simplest drinks to make. Just choose your favorite berries and mix it up and blend.

1 serving

INGREDIENTS	EQUIPMENT
1 cup ice cold milk	blender
½ cup berries	spoon
honey	measuring cup

1. Wash the berries and remove any stems (cut the stems from strawberries if you are using them).
2. Put the milk and the berries in the blender. Cover and blend on a high speed for 30 seconds.
3. Uncover the blender and taste, using the spoon. If it is not sweet enough for you, add some honey. Recover the blender and blend for 10 more seconds.
4. Pour and drink.

Carob Shake

This shake recipe is enough for two foamy glasses full of icy, chocolate-tasting goodness. **2 servings**

INGREDIENTS	EQUIPMENT
¾ cup milk	blender
¼ cup crushed ice cubes	heavy towel
¼ cup carob powder	hammer
2 tsp. honey	measuring cup
	measuring spoons

1. Crush the ice by wrapping some ice cubes in a heavy towel and smashing them a few times with a hammer.
2. Put all of the ingredients into the blender. Cover.
3. Blend on a high speed for one minute, and the shake is ready to drink.

Carob Energy Shake

All you need to make this shake is a large jar with a tight-fitting lid. **2 servings**

INGREDIENTS

2 cups milk

3 tbs. carob powder

2 tbs. honey

1 tbs. dry milk powder

½ tsp. vanilla

EQUIPMENT

1 large jar with lid

measuring cup

measuring spoons

1. Put all ingredients in the large jar. Cover tightly.
2. Shake the jar until all of the ingredients are well blended. This means that you have to shake it quite vigorously.
3. Pour and drink.

Banana Thick Shake

You don't need ice cream to make a thick, cold shake. If you have a blender, try this banana shake. **2 servings**

INGREDIENTS

1 banana, peeled and sliced

1 cup milk

1 tsp. honey

¼ tsp. nutmeg

½ cup cracked ice cubes

EQUIPMENT

blender

measuring cup

measuring spoons

knife for slicing banana

1. Put the milk, honey, banana, and ice cubes into the blender. Cover.
2. Blend at high speed for about 30 seconds.
3. Pour the shake into glasses and sprinkle with nutmeg.
4. Serve at once.

Banana-Orange Thick Shake

Here is a banana-orange shake that you can eat as a snack or drink for breakfast.

2 servings

INGREDIENTS	EQUIPMENT
2 ripe bananas, sliced	blender
1 tbs. honey	measuring spoons
1½ cups orange juice, ice cold	measuring cup

1. Put all of the ingredients in the blender and blend until they are smooth (about 30 seconds).
2. Serve immediately.

5

Parties: Dips and Other Treats

When you give a party, you like to think that your guests will really enjoy themselves. Part of the enjoyment rests with the kind of food you offer them to eat. Following chapters offer recipes for cakes, cookies, sandwiches, candy, and other party possibilities. This section will give you a few ideas about dips and other treats for you and your friends.

By all means combine the ideas in this book. Make some homemade crackers or bread to spread the dips on. Provide the necessary ingredients for homemade drinks and let your guests make their own concoctions. The goal of this section is to wean you away from those bags of chips in all flavors and packages of tasteless hotdog rolls.

You can make your parties as elaborate or as simple as you wish; you can spend an hour preparing the food or two days baking. In either case, introduce your friends to a healthy kind of snacking without even telling them you are doing it.

Mrs. De Palma's Pizza or "FICAGIO"

Mrs. DePalma lives in Hoboken, New Jersey, but she was born in Giovinazzo, Italy. Sitting in her kitchen is a happy experience. There always seems to be something simmering on the stove, baking in the oven, or pickling in jars on shelves. Like many European women, Mrs. DePalma uses no measuring tools or clocks when she cooks or bakes. To get this recipe, I sat with her and measured her handfuls of ingredients and timed the baking so that it could be shared with you.

Mrs. DePalma's Pizza is different from any store-bought or restaurant pizza I've eaten. It's also better. The recipe is probably hundreds of years old and has been passed from generation to generation without being written down. It's Italian name is *Ficagio* and it usually is not made with the gooey mozzarella cheese of ordinary pizzas. Why don't you make two—one Mrs. DePalma's way and one with mozzarella and decide for yourself which you like best.

One more piece of information: This is a very thick pizza. Mrs. DePalma's family often cuts a piece of cold pizza through the center and uses it as bread for delicious meat and cheese sandwiches.

INGREDIENTS	EQUIPMENT
3 cups unbleached flour	1 large plate
1 cake of yeast (or 1 envelope of yeast)	1 large knife
	1 small saucepan
3 medium-sized or 2 large potatoes	1 large saucepan
corn oil (or any vegetable or nut oil)	1 paring knife or potato peeler
	1 medium mixing bowl
½ cup water	potato masher or fork or potato ricer
2 level tbs. salt	

INGREDIENTS	EQUIPMENT
1 tbs. oregano	1 pizza pan or oblong baking pan
½ cup ground, peeled, canned to-	approximately 13 by 9 inches
matoes (or peeled whole canned	1 lightweight towel
tomatoes, mashed)	1 heavy towel
2 heaping tbs. grated parmesan or	measuring cup
romano cheese	measuring spoons
¼ lb. grated mozzarella cheese	
(optional)	

1. Peel the potatoes, cut them in quarters and place them in the large saucepan filled with water. Boil until a fork goes easily through them (about 20 to 25 minutes). Set aside.
2. Put ½ cup of water into the small saucepan with the salt. Heat over a low flame until *just* warm. Stir. Take the pan off the stove and add the yeast.
3. In the mixing bowl, mash the potatoes (or put them through a potato ricer). Set aside.
4. On a large clean surface, place the three cups of flour in a mound. (Mrs. DePalma has a huge pizza and noodle making board for this purpose. You can use a clean table or counter top.)
5. Make a large hole in the center of the flour and fill it with the mashed or riced potatoes.
6. Pour half of the warm yeast/water/salt mixture over the potatoes.
7. Using your hands, mix together the potato, flour, and liquid.
8. Add the rest of the water and begin kneading the dough (see chap. 11, p. 135 for instructions).
9. This is a sticky dough so keep sprinkling flour on your hands and on the surface of the counter or table.
10. After about five minutes, stop and scrape the dough

off the table surface and put it back into the main dough ball.

11. Continue kneading, sprinkling flour, and scraping the surface of the table for ten minutes more.

12. Make a ball out of the dough, flatten it slightly, and place it on a clean, dry, floured plate. If you are making more than one pizza (doubling or tripling the recipe), divide the dough at this point and set each dough ball on a clean, floured plate.

13. Dust the top of the dough with flour and place a lightweight towel or waxed paper over the dough. Place a heavy towel over the lightweight towel and set the dough in a warm, draught-free place for 1½ hours.

14. After the 1½ hours are up, preheat the oven to 350°.

15. Oil the pizza pan or the large baking dish very well—bottom and sides. Use 2 tablespoons of oil per pan.

16. Put the dough ball into the pan and spread it out gently with your fingers so it is spread evenly over the pan.

17. Gently rub 2 tablespoons of oil into the entire top surface of the dough with your fingers.

18. Pour the ½ cup of tomato onto the pizza and spread it gently over the entire surface with your fingers.

19. Sprinkle the tablespoon of oregano evenly over the top of the pizza.

20. Drip 2 more tablespoons of oil onto the top of the pizza—spreading it as evenly as possible. Try to avoid causing globs of oil in any one spot.

21. Bake at 350° for 20 minutes in the center of the oven. If you are making more than one pizza, place both shelves of the oven as close to the center as possible.

22. After 20 minutes, remove the pizza from the oven.

23. Sprinkle 2 tablespoons of parmesean or romano cheese

(or the ¼ pound of grated mozzarella cheese) evenly over the pizza.

24. Return to the oven and bake 15 minutes more or until the crust is golden brown. Lift a corner of the pizza with a knife and see if the bottom crust is also golden brown. If it isn't, return it to the oven for a few minutes.

25. If you are making more than one pizza, then switch them around the last 15 minutes of baking. Put the one that was on the top shelf on the bottom shelf and the one that baked on the bottom shelf onto the top shelf.

Let the pizza cool for at least ten minutes before eating to allow the flavor to sink in. This pizza is very good reheated.

Deviled Eggs

It's sometimes nice to have some solid food around for your guests to eat. Deviled eggs are delicious, filling and easy to make. This recipe makes 8 portions. You might want to make more. **8 servings**

INGREDIENTS	EQUIPMENT
4 eggs	1 medium saucepan
2 tbs. sour cream	1 sharp knife
¼ tsp. dry mustard	1 small mixing bowl
⅛ tsp. ground black pepper	1 fork
⅛ tsp. salt	1 large spoon
paprika	

1. Fill saucepan ½ full of water and bring it to a boil.
2. Lower the eggs into the boiling water and boil them for at least 10 minutes.
3. Remove the pan from the stove and hold it under the faucet in the sink. Run cold water into the pan.
4. When the eggs are cool enough to handle, remove them from the pot and set them aside for about 10 minutes.
5. Remove the shells from the eggs.
6. Cut each egg in half lengthwise.
7. Remove the yolks and put the yolks in the bowl.
8. Mash the yolks with a fork.
9. Add the mustard, sour cream, pepper, and salt to the yolks.
10. Mash some more until the mixture is smooth.
11. Put some of the egg yolk mixture back into each egg white half.
12. Sprinkle the filled eggs with paprika.
13. Refrigerate until you are ready to serve.

Roasted Almonds

Everyone likes to munch at a party. These almonds are a perfect munching food.

INGREDIENTS	EQUIPMENT
1¼ lbs. blanched almonds	1 large baking pan
¼ cup butter or margarine	1 large spoon for mixing
¼ cup soy sauce	measuring cup

1. Preheat oven to 375°F.
2. Place the almonds in the baking pan and spread them out as evenly as possible.

3. Bake them in the oven for about 15 minutes, stirring two or three times while they are baking.
4. Remove the pan from the oven.
5. Pour the soy sauce over the almonds and stir well.
6. Add the butter or margarine to the almonds. Stir well.
7. Return the almonds to the oven and bake them for another 12 to 15 minutes or until they are coated with soy sauce and just about dry. *Stir them every 3 minutes during the baking process.*
8. Remove them from the oven. Cool them completely.
9. Store the almonds in a covered container until you are ready to use them.

Cream Cheese Dips

Using a small bowl and a heavy spoon, you can blend cream cheese with a number of good things to make delicious dips. Here are some suggestions:

Cream cheese and olive dip:
Blend together about ⅓ cup of chopped olives and an 8 oz. package of cream cheese.
Cream cheese and onion dip:
Mince one medium onion and blend it with an 8 oz. package of cream cheese.
Cream cheese and clam dip:
Blend together 1 small can of drained, minced clams and an 8 oz. package of cream cheese. Blend in a dash of ground pepper and it is ready to serve.

Use your imagination and invent some cream cheese dips. If any of the above dips or any of the dips you invent seem to be a little too thick, thin them out by adding a tablespoon or two of milk.

Fruit Treats

There is no recipe for this party snack. Simply choose your favorite fruits which will do well unrefrigerated, push them onto toothpicks and arrange them on a large platter.

Some examples are a grape, chunk of pineapple, and a strawberry on one pick and an orange section, a chunk of fresh peach, and a pitted cherry on another pick.

If you don't have time to put the fruit on the picks, then simply arrange a platter of mixed fruit and chunks of fruit and leave the toothpicks next to it.

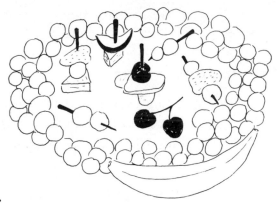

Candy Apples

Before you decide to make this party snack, you will have to find a supply of clean sticks which are about the length of a pencil to insert in the apples.

INGREDIENTS	EQUIPMENT
apples (as many as you think will be eaten)	1 large platter
⅛ cup of honey per apple	2 medium mixing bowls
ground walnuts or pecans (½ lb. = 1⅓ cups)	enough sticks to go with the apples

---

1. Pour the honey into one mixing bowl.
2. Pour the ground nuts into the other mixing bowl.
3. Insert a stick into the center of each apple so the apples can be lifted by the sticks.
4. Dip each apple in the honey, making sure that the honey covers every part of the apple.
5. Hold the apple over the honey bowl for a minute and let the excess honey drip off.
6. Roll the apple in the dish of ground nuts so that it gets completely covered with a layer of nuts.
7. Place the apple on the platter.
8. Keep repeating steps 4 through 7 until all the apples are coated.
9. Refrigerate until ready to serve.

Spicy Cheese Dip

Place a platter of raw carrots, sliced mushrooms, celery, and tiny pieces of cauliflower next to this dip. **About 2 cups**

INGREDIENTS	EQUIPMENT
1 4 oz. package of cream cheese, softened	1 medium mixing bowl
1 pt. sour cream	1 heavy spoon for creaming
¼ tsp. curry powder	
¼ tsp. ground pepper	
½ tsp. lemon juice	
1 tsp. dried parsley	

1. Cream the cream cheese until it is soft.
2. Slowly add the sour cream and thoroughly blend the two together.
3. Add all other ingredients and mix well.
4. Refrigerate until ready to serve.

VARIATIONS:

Try substituting 2 tsp. of chopped chives for the curry powder. If you like onion, chop one small onion into tiny pieces and use it instead of the curry powder.

Guacamole

Try to get a taste of this dip in the kitchen because it rarely lasts long once it has been put on the table.

About 1 ½ cups

INGREDIENTS	EQUIPMENT
2 ripe avocados	1 medium mixing bowl
2 tbs. lemon or lime juice	1 fork
1 ½ tsp. salt	1 knife
1 tsp. ground black pepper	measuring spoons
1 clove of garlic, crushed	1 garlic crusher (if you don't have
¼ cup chopped scallions or onion	one, then mince the clove of
1 tomato, cubed	garlic)
8 or 10 black olives	

1. Peel and mash the avocados thoroughly in the mixing bowl.
2. Add the salt, pepper, garlic, and lemon or lime juice to the mashed avocado. Mix thoroughly.
3. Using your fork, vigorously stir in the chopped scallions or onion.

4. Spoon the guacamole into a pretty dish and garnish with the cubed tomato and the olives.
5. Refrigerate until you are ready to serve.

Salmon Dip

This dip is best if it is made in a blender. If you don't have a blender and you want to make it, try to mash the salmon until it is smooth before adding the other ingredients.

About 2 cups

INGREDIENTS

1 7¾ oz. can of salmon, drained

3 drops of tabasco sauce

1 tbs. chives (dried is fine)

½ tsp. paprika

1 tsp. dried parsley flakes

⅛ tsp. ground pepper

dash of salt

1 pt. plain yoghurt

EQUIPMENT

blender

measuring spoons

---

1. Put all ingredients in the blender and cover.
2. Blend on the high speed for about 30 to 40 seconds.
3. You may have to turn off the blender after about 15 seconds to stir the mixture. DO NOT TRY STIRRING THE DIP WHILE THE BLENDER IS TURNED ON.

Noodle Kugel

Parties and holidays always remind me of my grandmother's kugels (puddings). They are filling and so delicious that I never remember seeing any leftovers.

8 servings

INGREDIENTS	EQUIPMENT
3 eggs	egg beater or electric mixer
4 tbs. honey	1 large mixing bowl
4 cups cooked, broad noodles	1 medium baking dish (preferably
½ cup raisins	glass)
½ cup sliced, blanched almonds	1 large spoon for mixing
or chopped walnuts	1 large pot for cooking noodles
4 tbs. melted butter or margarine	1 small saucepan for melting butter
⅛ tsp. nutmeg	pastry brush
1 tbs. lemon juice	
2 tbs. bread crumbs (unflavored)	
some extra honey	

1. Cook noodles according to the instructions on the package. Drain and set aside.
2. Preheat oven to 375° F.
3. In the large mixing bowl, beat the eggs and 4 tbs. of honey until they are fluffy.
4. Add the raisins, nutmeg, nuts, lemon juice, and melted butter or margarine. Stir well.
5. Grease the baking dish.
6. Add the noodles to the mixture in the mixing bowl and stir well.
7. Pour the noodle mixture into the baking dish.
8. Brush the top of the noodle mixture with the extra honey.
9. Sprinkle the top of the pudding with bread crumbs.
10. Bake for 50 minutes at 375° or until the pudding is brown on top.
11. Serve warm with fruit compote, poached fruit, or just plain.

Potato Kugel

Here is another pudding I remember eating at my grandmother's house. Serve it with other hot food such as hamburgers, hotdogs, chicken, or as a side dish to platters of tuna salad and egg salad.   **About 6 servings**

INGREDIENTS

3 eggs

3 cups grated potatoes, drained

⅓ cup potato flour or unbleached
 white flour

½ tsp. baking powder

4 tbs. melted butter or margarine

3 tbs. grated onion

⅛ tsp. pepper

1½ tsp. salt

EQUIPMENT

grater (or blender)

1 large mixing bowl

1 medium mixing bowl

1 small mixing bowl

1 8x8-inch glass baking pan or a
 1½ qt. casserole

sieve

measuring cup

measuring spoons

1 small saucepan for melting butter
 or margarine

1 large spoon for mixing

1. Preheat oven to 350° F.
2. Grate the onion into the small mixing bowl and set aside.
3. Peel and grate the potatoes into the medium mixing bowl, dump them into the sieve over the sink and drain. If you have a blender, cut up the potatoes into small chunks and blend them in the blender until they are smooth. Pour into the sieve and drain.
4. In the large mixing bowl, beat the eggs until they are quite thick.

5. Add the drained potatoes, flour, onion, baking powder, salt, pepper, and melted butter or margarine to the eggs.
6. Stir the mixture until it is thoroughly blended.
7. Grease your casserole dish or baking pan.
8. Spoon the pudding mixture into the pan.
9. Bake at 350° for about 1 hour or until the pudding is brown on top. Serve hot.

You can make this and the noodle kugel the day before and reheat them before serving.

6

Candies

You usually eat candy as a quick snack going to or coming from school, during a break in exercise for quick energy, while sitting in the movies, while watching television or, sometimes, in place of a missed breakfast or lunch. The problem with candy is that it is so easy to get and so easy to carry around that it's hard to resist.

You'll understand why candy eating is a problem if you read the list of ingredients on some candy wrappers— chocolate, caramel (melted sugar), sugar, chemical preservatives, and other flavorings—usually artificial. Occasionally you will find some fruit or nuts in a piece of candy. For the most part candy offers you no nutrition, is bad for your teeth and skin, and only provides you with a very short-lived spurt of energy.

However, candy wasn't always so available to people and it wasn't always made by assembly-line machines and filled with chemicals and artificial ingredients. The earliest kind of candy we know about came from the Orient and was made of preserved or candied fruits—probably sweetened with honey.

In the Western world, the earliest function of candy was not for pleasure eating. During medieval times, physicians made a candy of gum dragon, white sugar, and rosewater which was beaten into a paste. This was called sugarplate and it was mixed with unpleasant medicine to disguise the taste.

During the same period of time, some candy eaten on special occasions came into being. One kind of this early candy is still eaten today—a simple confection that was and is known throughout Europe—marchpane or marzipan. It's made of almonds, pistachios, or other nuts which have been ground into a paste and mixed with sugar and egg white. Today, as in the Middle Ages, marzipan is often molded into fancy shapes and stamped with designs and, for many people, is still considered a holiday candy.

By the seventeenth century, candymaking became a more widespread skill and inventions such as the sugarplum (made of boiled sugar) came into existence. However, it wasn't until the nineteenth century that candy became available to most people year round. In 1851, there was an international exhibition in Europe (much like a World's Fair) and one of the more popular exhibits included English boiled sweets (candy). People were so delighted by these sweets that the manufacture of candy spread quickly throughout Europe and the United States. By the middle of the nineteenth century, there were approximately 380 small candy factories in the United States making lozenges, jujube paste, and stock candy (candy sticks and jaw breakers). Most of the fine and fancy candy was imported.

Over the years, modern machinery developed and candymaking became a big business. Most candy today is made in huge quantities by complicated machines. It is usually mostly sugar in some form and chocolate plus the usual preservatives and chemicals.

This doesn't mean that you should stop eating candy. Instead of depriving yourself, you can make your own candy. The difference is that the candy you make will be made of honey instead of sugar, carob instead of chocolate, and fresh nuts and dried fruits instead of the soggy, stale-tasting equivalents you usually find in store-bought candy.

You can be quite creative with your candymaking by using the kind of nuts and fruits and honey you like best. The results will be sweet candy to carry around that will also be healthy food.

Honey Drop Candies

These honey candies are not only simple to make but have a very, very long history. They were originally made in clean, firmly packed snow instead of on crushed ice. In fact, you can still make them on snow during the winter. Simply fill a large bowl with clean, packed snow, carry it inside and make your candies. **About 5 dozen**

INGREDIENTS	EQUIPMENT
1 cup of your favorite honey	1 large bowl
½ cup water	1 tableware teaspoon
1 large bowl of firmly packed crushed ice, or firmly packed clean snow	1 medium saucepan
	cellophane wrap
	measuring cup

1. You can crush your ice by wrapping ice cubes in a heavy towel and banging them with a hammer. Make sure that you have at least four trays full of ice cubes. If the ice seems to be melting down, drain off the water and add more crushed ice (or snow).
2. Pour the honey and the water in the saucepan and heat it until it boils.
3. Keep the mixture boiling for fifteen minutes.
4. Turn down the heat a bit.
5. Take a spoonful of the boiling liquid and drop it on the ice. It will become solid immediately.
6. Drop about three more spoonsful of honey on the ice and quickly remove the hardened candies to a dish.
7. Continue making small batches of this candy, occasionally turning the heat up under the pot for a minute or so to keep the temperature up.
8. When all of the candies are made, wrap each one in a tiny piece of cellophane wrap.
9. You can keep these candies on a shelf, in a candy dish, or in a jar.

Marzipan

It was mentioned in the introduction to this chapter that marzipan is one of the oldest known candies in the Western world. The original marzipan was made with much sugar; as a matter of fact, most marzipan today is made with great amounts of sugar. The following is a slight variation on this old candy. I hope you enjoy it.

About 5 dozen small or 3 dozen large candies

½ lb. ground almonds (or walnuts
    if your local market does not sell
    ground almonds)
honey

1 heavy spoon
1 medium mixing bowl
cellophane wrap

1. Pour the ground nuts into the mixing bowl.
2. Add a little honey and begin mashing the mixture against the side of the bowl.
3. Add a little more honey and mash and mix some more.
4. Continue doing this until you have a thick paste made of nuts and honey.
5. With your hands, knead and squeeze this paste for a minute or two and then shape the marzipan into candies —large or small.
6. Wrap each candy in cellophane wrap and refrigerate if you wish. Refrigeration will produce a chewier candy. Storage outside of the refrigerator will produce a softer candy.

Easy Peanut Butter Candy

Here is rich peanut butter candy which is very simple.

About 14 candies

INGREDIENTS

EQUIPMENT

⅓ cup honey
⅓ cup peanut butter
¼ cup toasted wheat germ
½ cup dry milk powder
¼ cup chopped peanuts

1 large knife for chopping
1 board for chopping
1 large mixing bowl
1 heavy spoon for creaming
measuring cup
cellophane wrap

1. If your wheat germ is not toasted, toast it in a 350° F. oven for 10 to 15 minutes or until it is lightly brown.
2. In the mixing bowl, combine the honey and peanut butter and cream until smooth with the heavy spoon.
3. Add the wheat germ and mix it in thoroughly.
4. Add the milk powder and mix it in thoroughly.
5. Dump the peanuts into the bowl and work them into the candy with your fingers until they are thoroughly mixed in.
6. Roll the candy into a sausage shape which is approximately ¾ inch thick. Use your hands and the board to do this on. Do it gently or the candy will stick to the board and to you.
7. Cut the candy roll into 1-inch pieces and wrap each one in cellophane wrap.
8. This recipe makes quite a bit of candy. Store it in a covered container.
9. If you like really chewy candy, store it in the refrigerator.

Peanut Butter Candies

You can make a batch of these gooey candies in about 15 minutes—which is a good thing because you will probably want to make a second batch after finishing the first.

12–15 candies

INGREDIENTS	EQUIPMENT
½ cup peanut butter	1 large mixing bowl
½ cup sesame seeds	several small baking pans for toasting seeds and wheat germ
¼ cup raisins	
¼ cup shelled peanuts	measuring cup

INGREDIENTS	EQUIPMENT
4 tbs. honey	measuring spoons
1 tsp. lemon extract	cellophane wrap
¼ cup wheat germ	1 heavy spoon for creaming
¼ cup ground almonds or walnuts	1 small dish for ground almonds

1. If you have untoasted sesame seeds and/or untoasted wheat germ, put each ingredient in a small baking pan and bake for 10 to 15 minutes at 350° F. or until lightly brown. If your sesame seeds and wheat germ are toasted, begin with step 2.
2. In the large mixing bowl, cream together the honey and the peanut butter until they are smooth.
3. Add the lemon extract and cream it until thoroughly blended.
4. Add the sesame seeds, raisins, peanuts, and wheat germ. Mix them thoroughly until all are coated with peanut butter.
5. With your hands, form the candy mixture into 12 to 15 balls.
6. Roll each ball in the ground almonds or walnuts (you can buy these ground in the supermarket) and wrap each piece of candy in cellophane wrap.
7. These candies do not have to be refrigerated.

No-Cook Carob or Peanut Butter Fudge

Here is an easy fudge for you to make which is both soft and chewy, and crunchy. You can use carob powder for a chocolate-flavored fudge or peanut butter. When you buy your sunflower seeds for this recipe, try to get them shelled.

To begin by shelling ½ cup of sunflower seeds might take much of the pleasure out of this fudge.

About 6 dozen small candies

INGREDIENTS

½ cup dry, nonfat milk powder

½ cup peanut butter or carob powder

½ cup chopped walnuts

½ cup sunflower seeds

½ cup sesame seeds

1 cup shredded coconut, unsweetened

¼ cup honey

¼ cup water

butter or margarine for greasing pan

EQUIPMENT

1 large mixing bowl

1 large spoon for mixing

1 9x9-inch baking pan

measuring cup

1 small, sharp knife

cellophane wrap

1. Grease the baking pan and set it aside.
2. Put the milk powder, peanut butter *or* carob powder, honey, and water into the mixing bowl. Blend together well.
3. Add the sesame seeds and the sunflower seeds and mix in well.
4. Add the chopped walnuts and the coconut. Mix well until all the ingredients are blended well and are sticking together.
5. Spoon the fudge into the greased baking pan and press it down so that it covers the entire pan.
6. Cut the fudge into squares and wrap each one individually. Store in a covered container or in the refrigerator if you like chewy candy.

Mixed-Fruit Candy Balls

These nutty, chewy candies offer a great energy lift to the snacker. If you have a blender, the job of making them will be simplified. If you don't, a little more time will be involved in the making but the results will be the same.

About 36 candy balls

INGREDIENTS	EQUIPMENT
½ cup raisins	3 small baking pans for toasting nuts
½ cup pitted dates	
½ cup figs	1 large knife for chopping
½ cup pitted prunes	1 board for chopping
½ cup chopped nuts	blender or food grinder (optional)
1 orange, peeled and seeded	1 large mixing bowl
⅓ cup wheat germ	1 large spoon for mixing
½ tsp. cinnamon	measuring cup
¼ cup sesame seeds	measuring spoons
¼ cup almonds, sliced	

1. Preheat the oven to 350° F.
2. Put the sliced almonds in one small baking pan, the sesame seed in another, and the wheat germ in the third (if your wheat germ is raw). If your wheat germ is toasted, do not roast it again.
3. Place the pans in the oven and bake until the nuts, seeds, and wheat germ are light brown (10 to 15 minutes). Remove from oven and cool.
4. Chop the raisins, figs, dates, prunes, and orange slices into very, very tiny pieces. If you have a blender, put them in the blender and blend (with the cover on) for about a minute. If you have a food grinder, put these ingredients through the grinder.

5. When the above ingredients are finely chopped, put them in the large mixing bowl.
6. Add the toasted wheat germ and the cinnamon and mix together thoroughly with the large spoon.
7. With your hands, shape 36 tightly packed candy balls from the mixture.
8. Roll half of the balls in the sesame seeds and half of them in the toasted almonds.
9. Refrigerate until you are ready to eat.

Halvah

Halvah is an ancient Middle Eastern candy which traveled the world with various conquests and explorations. This is, of course, a modern version of the old candy but its unique texture and taste are fairly authentic.

INGREDIENTS: Candy	EQUIPMENT
¾ cup margarine or butter, room temperature	1 heavy spoon for creaming
2 cups quick-cooking farina cereal	1 large mixing bowl
1 cup honey	egg beater or electric mixer
4 eggs	1 medium saucepan
1 cup blanched almonds, chopped	1 9x5x3-inch loaf pan or 1 8-inch square baking pan
1 tsp. cinnamon	measuring cup
INGREDIENTS: Syrup	measuring spoons
2 cups honey	1 large knife for chopping nuts
1 1-inch cinnamon stick	
1 cup water	

1. Preheat oven to 350° F.
2. Grease the loaf pan or the baking pan. The loaf pan will give you a higher candy and the baking pan will produce a flatter candy.
3. In the mixing bowl, cream together the margarine and the honey.
4. When the mixture is smooth, beat in the eggs one at a time.
5. Keep beating the mixture after all of the eggs are added until it is very light and frothy.
6. Add the uncooked farina and stir well.
7. Add the nuts and ground cinnamon and stir well.
8. Pour the candy batter into the greased pan.
9. For the 9x5x3-inch loaf pan: Bake for 40 minutes or until done. For the 8x8-inch baking pan: Bake for 25 to 30 minutes or until done.
10. Test for doneness: insert the tip of a dry, clean table knife into the center of the candy. If it comes out clean, it is done.
11. About 10 minutes before the halvah has finished baking, pour the 2 cups of honey and the cup of water into the saucepan. Put in the stick of cinnamon.
12. Cook the honey and water and cinnamon stick over a medium flame for about 7 to 10 minutes, stirring occasionally.
13. When the halvah is baked, remove it from the oven.
14. Immediately pour the hot honey/water syrup over the halvah, distributing it as evenly as possible.
15. Discard the stick of cinnamon.
16. Let the halvah cool thoroughly in its pan.
17. When it is cooled, cut it into small squares. You can wrap each square individually in cellophane wrap or store them in a covered container. Since they are sticky, individual wrapping may be a better idea.

Fruit Bars

A blender is useful in making these fruit bars but, with a little energy, you can make them without one. This is a naturally sweet treat that is packed with energy.

About 10 bars

INGREDIENTS

1 lb. figs or pitted dates

2 cups finely chopped or ground almonds or unsalted walnuts

⅓ cup shredded, unsweetened coconut

½ cup raisins

EQUIPMENT

blender, food grinder, or large, sharp knife

chopping board if you are using the knife

rolling pin

waxed paper

cellophane wrap

1 small, sharp knife

measuring cup

---

1. If you have a blender or food grinder, put the figs or dates, raisins, and nuts in it. Blend or grind all ingredients together.
2. If you do not have a blender or grinder, then mince the figs or dates and the raisins. Buy finely chopped or ground nuts if you can or you will have to mince the nuts, too.
3. Spread a large piece of waxed paper on a counter or table top and put the fruit and nuts in the center of it.
4. Work the fruit and nuts into a tightly packed ball with your hands, making sure, if you've chopped them with a knife, that they are well mixed and are sticking together.
5. Flatten the ball slightly and cover it with another sheet of waxed paper.

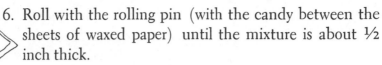

6. Roll with the rolling pin (with the candy between the sheets of waxed paper) until the mixture is about ½ inch thick.
7. Peel off the top sheet of waxed paper.
8. Cut the rolled candy into bars (about 1½ by 3½ inches).
9. Press the shredded coconut into all surfaces of the candy bars.
10. Wrap each candy bar in cellophane wrap and store in a covered container.

Honey Marshmallows

Store-bought marshmallows are mostly sugar; this recipe is mostly honey. You will have to make it the day before you want to eat it because it must stand overnight. However, the results are well worth the wait.

About 6½ dozen

INGREDIENTS	EQUIPMENT
1 cup honey	1 double boiler
1 tbs. unflavored gelatin	1 small saucepan
¼ cup cold water	egg beater or electric mixer
¾ lb. shredded, unsweetened coconut	1 9x9-inch glass baking pan
	1 small sharp knife
	rolling pin
	cookie sheet or large baking pan
	1 large sheet of plain brown paper (a large paper bag)
	1 medium mixing bowl

First Day:

1. In the top of the double boiler, soak the gelatin in the cold water.
2. Turn on the heat under the double boiler (be sure to put at least a cup of water in the bottom of the double boiler) and dissolve the gelatin further over hot water. When it is fully dissolved, turn off the heat.
3. Put the honey in the small saucepan and warm it for about 1½ minutes over a medium flame.
4. Pour the honey and the gelatin into the medium mixing bowl.
5. With the egg beater or the electric mixer, beat the gelatin/honey mixture until it is light and fluffy. This will take a great deal of beating—from 10 to 20 minutes.
6. When the mixture is light and fluffy, grease the 9x9-inch glass baking pan.
7. Turn the mixture into the pan and gently spread it out so that it is smooth.
8. Lay a sheet of tin foil or waxed paper loosely over the top of the pan and let it stand for 24 to 48 hours.

Second or Third Day:

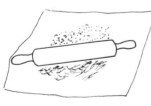

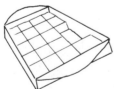

1. Dip the small, sharp knife in cold water and cut the marshmallows into squares.
2. Spread the coconut on the cookie sheet or in the large baking pan.
3. Heat the oven to 350° F. and bake the coconut until it is lightly browned.
4. Cool the coconut and then spread it on the large piece of brown paper.
5. Roll the coconut with the rolling pin so that it is broken into tiny, fine bits.
6. Lift the marshmallows out of their pan one by one and roll each one in the coconut.
7. Store these candies in an airtight container until they are ready to be eaten.

Cracker Jacks

Commercial Cracker Jacks are made with a great deal of caramel which is simply melted sugar. These Cracker Jacks are just as good and are made with honey, fresh nuts, and popcorn. The only thing that you'll miss out on if you make this recipe yourself is the prize in the box. Double the recipe if you are sharing this with family or friends.

About 1½ quarts

INGREDIENTS

¼ cup honey
¼ cup butter or margarine
1½ qts. popped popcorn
¾ cup peanuts, shelled

EQUIPMENT

1 2 or 3 qt. pot, with a lid for popping popcorn, or a popcorn popper
1 very large mixing bowl
1 cookie sheet or large baking pan
1 large spoon for mixing
1 small saucepan
measuring cup

1. Pop your popcorn in a popcorn popper or in the 2 to 3 quart pot according to the directions on the jar or can of popping corn.
2. Preheat your oven to 350° F.
3. In the small saucepan, mix together the honey and the margarine or butter. Heat it over a low heat until it is blended together. Stir it occasionally.
4. Place the popped corn and the peanuts in a large bowl and mix them together.
5. Slowly pour the honey/margarine or honey/butter mixture over the popcorn/nut mixture, stirring as you pour.
6. When all of the honey mixture is poured into the bowl,

mix the popcorn and peanut mixture very well so that all of it gets covered with the honey mixture.

7. Spread the popcorn/nut mixture in a single layer on a cookie sheet or in a large baking pan. You will have to make several batches unless you have several cookie sheets or baking pans.

8. Bake for 10 to 15 minutes at 350° or until the cracker jacks are crisp.

9. Cool them in a large, clean bowl and store them in a covered container.

7

Puddings, Custards, and Whips

Pudding

Pudding is a very old food which has changed through the years as cooking equipment and the availability of ingredients have changed. The earliest kind of pudding was boiled in a bag or cloth. Later, as cooking became a more advanced art, puddings were put in buttered bowls or dishes, covered with cloths, and steamed. Modern puddings are either steamed, baked, or simply chilled in a refrigerator.

Today there are puddings that are cooked and served with meat, puddings served as sweets and desserts, and puddings made from a wide variety of ingredients such as milk, rice, breadcrumbs, and dried and fresh fruit.

Custard

Custard is a form of pudding. The word "custard" comes from a Latin verb *crustare* which means "to crust." Custards are usually made of milk, eggs, sweetening, and flavoring; they can be baked or boiled. A nice thing about custard is that it can be eaten plain or used to fill pies, the layers between cakes, or the insides of pastries such as éclairs.

Whips

Whips are modern inventions that have become popular with modern kitchen equipment. A frothy whip (usually a blend of fruit, whipped cream, flavoring, and sweetener) depends upon very vigorous beating. If you have a blender or an electric mixer, whips will be easy to make. If not, a hand egg beater will work for many of the recipes with a little more effort on your part.

The whips in this chapter make delicious desserts and snacks as well as good icings and fillings for cakes and cupcakes. They also offer the most opportunity for exercising your imagination. Once you master the technique of making a whip, begin experimenting with different fruits and spices.

Custard Cups

Puddings and custards are often made in small, heat-resistant cups called custard cups. These earthenware or glass cups can be put in an oven or in a steamer. They have no handles and often come with their own lids so that they can be refrigerated, kept fresh, and later used as individual serving dishes.

Custard cups are also ideal for making baked apples, miniature pies, and other desserts that need oven cooking. However, they are not absolutely necessary for you to have.

Any dessert that can be baked or steamed in a custard cup, can be made in a larger, heat-resistant container.

Always Use Glass

Don't make your puddings and custards in metal baking dishes. Metal containers do something unpleasant to the taste of a baking or steaming pudding or custard. Use a heat-resistant glass or earthenware casserole or baking dish.

Plain Egg Custard

This recipe may be called "plain" egg custard but it is an extremely versatile and delicious snack. It is great for breakfast if you like something sweet in the morning, but feel that you should eat an egg (a good idea), or it makes a fine dessert or snack especially when topped with whipped cream.

6 servings

INGREDIENTS	EQUIPMENT
5 eggs	egg beater or electric mixer
¾ cup honey	1 large mixing bowl
2 cups milk	1 glass oven-proof casserole or 6 individual custard cups
2 tsp. vanilla	
½ tsp. nutmeg	1 large baking pan (large enough to hold the casserole or the six custard cups)
pinch of cloves (ground)	
cinnamon	
	measuring spoons
	measuring cup

1. Preheat oven to 350° F.
2. In the large mixing bowl, beat the eggs until they are light, fluffy, and lemon-colored.
3. Add the honey and vanilla and beat well.
4. Slowly add the milk, beating constantly.
5. Add the nutmeg and pinch of cloves and beat.
6. Pour the custard into the glass casserole dish or equally into the six custard cups.
7. Sprinkle the top of the custard with cinnamon.
8. Pull the shelf of your oven out a bit and place the large baking pan on it.
9. Place the six custard cups filled with custard or the casserole filled with custard in the baking pan.
10. Pour enough hot water into the pan so that the water is one inch deep around the cups or casserole.
11. Gently push the shelf back into place and bake for 30 minutes at 350° or until done. (If you are *using individual cups*, bake for *only 15 minutes*).
12. Do not overcook your custard. You can tell if it's done because the custard will be light brown on top and slightly soft in the center when it is ready to be removed from the oven.
13. Cool and then chill. Serve chilled and store it in the refrigerator.

Orange Custard

Here is an unusual custard that is very easy to make. Serve it cold, topped with whipped cream or simply as it is.

6 servings

INGREDIENTS	EQUIPMENT
grated rind of 1 orange	grater
½ cup honey	1 medium saucepan

INGREDIENTS	EQUIPMENT
3 cups milk	*1 large spoon for mixing*
3 tbs. cornstarch	*1 large mixing bowl*
3 egg yolks, slightly beaten	*egg beater or electric mixer*
3 tsp. honey	*6 custard cups or dessert dishes*

1. Put milk, ½ cup of honey, grated orange rind, and cornstarch into the saucepan and stir very well.
2. Cook the above mixture over a low heat, stirring it constantly until it has thickened.
3. When the custard has thickened (so that it is quite thick and creamy), remove it from the heat.
4. Pour the custard into a large mixing bowl and beat in the three yolks with the egg beater or electric mixer.
5. When the egg yolks are thoroughly blended into the custard, spoon the custard into 6 individual custard cups or dessert dishes.
6. Chill in the refrigerator for 15 minutes.
7. Remove from the refrigerator and pour ½ teaspoon of honey over each custard. Return to the refrigerator and chill until ready to serve.

Fruit Custard

You can use any kind of dried or fresh fruit for this custard. If you use dried fruit, soak it in warm water until it is soft before using it and then drain it in a sieve. If you use fresh fruit with edible skins (such as apples or peaches), do not peel them. The nicest kind of fruit custard is made with mixed fruit such as apples and raisins or apricots (dried or fresh) and peaches.

6 servings

INGREDIENTS

1½ cups hot milk

2 eggs

2 tbs. honey

⅔ cup diced raw or dried (see instructions above) fruit

cinnamon

butter or margarine

EQUIPMENT

1 small saucepan

1 large mixing bowl

1 large knife for dicing fruit

egg beater or electric mixer

glass oven-proof casserole or 6 custard cups

1 large baking pan (large enough to hold the casserole or the six custard cups)

1 large spoon

measuring cup

measuring spoons

1. Preheat oven to 325° F.
2. Pour the milk into the saucepan and heat it over a medium flame until it is hot. Set it aside.
3. In the mixing bowl, beat together the eggs and the honey until the mixture is light and foamy.
4. Slowly add the hot milk to the honey/egg mixture and beat constantly.
5. After all of the milk has been beaten into the mixture, add the fruit and stir well.
6. Lightly butter the custard cups or casserole.
7. Beat the custard with a spoon for about one more minute and spoon it into the custard cups or casserole. Sprinkle with cinnamon.
8. Pull the shelf of your oven out a bit.
9. Place the large baking pan on the shelf and place the cups or casserole into the pan.
10. Pour some water into the pan so that it is about 1 inch deep around the custard cups or casserole.

Puddings, Custards, and Whips

86

11. Gently push the oven shelf back into place.
12. Bake the custard for about 20 minutes (for the custard cups) or about 30 minutes (for the casserole) at 325° or until the top of the custard is light brown and the custard is soft only in the center.
13. Cool on a counter and then refrigerate.

Chinese Almond Pudding

I usually make this recipe in double or triple proportions because people love it so much. I have never had any leftovers for private snacking the next day. Top this pudding with canned or fresh pineapple chunks or tiny mandarin oranges (now available in cans packed in their own juice). Serve it in a large bowl and spoon it out at the table because it is really pretty to look at as well as delicious.

4 servings

INGREDIENTS	EQUIPMENT
¾ cup (1 small can) evaporated milk	1 large saucepan
1 envelope (1 tbs.) unflavored gelatin	1 small bowl
1¼ cups cold water	1 large serving bowl
1 tbs. almond extract	1 large spoon for mixing
6 tbs. honey	measuring cup
3 tbs. water	measuring spoons
pineapple chunks or mandarin oranges	

1. In the small bowl, dissolve the gelatin in the 3 table-spoons of water and set it aside.
2. Pour the evaporated milk and the 1¼ cups of water into the saucepan. Stir well.
3. Add the honey to the milk mixture and heat the milk/honey/water mixture to just below boiling. Stir occasionally.
4. Turn off the heat and add the almond extract. Stir in well.
5. Add the dissolved gelatin and stir in very well.
6. Pour the liquid into a large serving bowl and let it cool for about 15 minutes.
7. Place the bowl in the refrigerator until the pudding sets. This will take several hours.
8. Serve with the mandarin and/or pineapple chunks arranged nicely on top of the pudding.

Baked Fruit Pudding

Baked fruit pudding combines the flavor and texture of pudding with the flavor and texture of baked fruit. Use apples or peaches for this pudding and serve it plain or heaped with whipped cream. **6 servings**

INGREDIENTS	EQUIPMENT
4 apples or peaches	1 paring knife
⅔ cup milk	1 large knife for slicing
2 cups flour	1 large mixing bowl
2 tsp. baking powder	1 large spoon for mixing
½ tsp. salt	1 glass baking dish 9x9 inches

½ cup honey   measuring cup

1 egg, well beaten   measuring spoons

2 tbs. melted butter or margarine   pastry brush

honey   1 small dish for beaten egg

cinnamon   1 fork for beating egg

                               small saucepan for melting butter

1. Preheat oven to 350° F.
2. Peel, core, and slice apples. (For peaches, simply remove the pit and slice, do not peel).
3. Grease the baking dish.
4. Arrange all of the fruit on the bottom of the baking pan.
5. Brush the fruit with honey and sprinkle it with cinnamon.
6. In the mixing bowl, combine the flour, baking powder, salt, ½ cup honey, beaten egg, melted butter or margine, and milk.
7. Stir the mixture well until you have a smooth batter.
8. Pour the batter over the fruit.
9. Bake at 350° for ½ hour or until done (a toothpick will come out clean).
10. Serve warm and use the baking pan as a serving dish.

Rice Pudding

Use real rice for your homemade rice pudding. Do not use any of the quick-cooking varieties. This recipe will serve about six people (or four hungry people) and is better than any store-bought rice pudding I've eaten. **6 servings**

INGREDIENTS

3 cups milk

1 cup light or heavy cream

1 cinnamon stick, 2 to 3 inches long

2 strips of lemon rind (yellow part only)

2 strips of orange rind (orange part only)

1 cup uncooked rice

2 cups water

⅔ cup honey

¼ tsp. vanilla

1 cup raisins

ground cinnamon

EQUIPMENT

1 large, heavy saucepan with lid

1 medium saucepan

1 large spoon for mixing

1 large, oven-proof casserole (must hold at least 1 quart)

measuring cup

measuring spoons

sieve

1. In the medium saucepan, boil the 2 cups of water.
2. When the water is boiling, add the cup of rice and boil for 5 minutes.
3. Remove the rice from the heat and, over the sink, dump it in the sieve and drain it well. Set it aside.
4. In the large saucepan, place the milk, cream, cinnamon stick, orange rind, and lemon rind.
5. Place the large saucepan on the stove and turn on the heat to moderately low.
6. When the milk/cream mixture begins to gently boil, add the rice to it, stir it well and turn down the heat to low.
7. Put the lid on the saucepan, leaving it a bit askew so that the top of the saucepan is not totally covered.
8. Simmer the rice/milk/cream mixture for 15 minutes, stirring every 3 minutes or so.

9. Add the honey and raisins, replace the lid (askew), and let it simmer for another 15 to 20 minutes, stirring occasionally.
10. When the rice is very soft and most of the liquid is absorbed, remove from the heat.
11. Stir in the vanilla.
12. Spoon the rice pudding into a buttered, oven-proof 1 quart (or larger) casserole dish. Dust the top with cinnamon and chill for at least 2 hours. Remove the rinds and cinnamon stick just before serving.

Bread Pudding

Bread pudding is a practical and delicious way to use up stale, leftover bread. Any kind of bread will do for this pudding because each bread adds new flavor to the pudding. **6 servings**

INGREDIENTS	EQUIPMENT
6 slices of stale bread	1 large knife
butter or margarine	1 medium mixing bowl
cinnamon	1 small bowl for beaten eggs
¾ cup honey	1 fork for beating eggs
¾ cup raisins	1 large spoon for mixing
4 eggs, lightly beaten	1 1½ qt. baking dish (glass)
2 cups milk	1 large baking pan (large enough
1 tsp. vanilla	so baking dish can fit into it)
1 tbs. grated lemon rind	measuring cup
2 tbs. honey for topping	measuring spoons
	1 table knife
	1 small mixing bowl

1. Preheat oven to 375° F.
2. Lightly toast the 6 slices of bread.
3. With the table knife, spread a good amount of margarine or butter on each piece of bread.
4. In the small mixing bowl, combine ¼ cup of the honey with a few dashes of cinnamon. Mix well.
5. Spread the honey/cinnamon mixture on the bread.
6. Make 3 sandwiches out of the 6 slices of bread.
7. Cut each sandwich into long, fingerlike pieces.
8. Grease your glass baking dish and place the sandwich pieces in it.
9. Spread the remaining honey over the sandwich pieces, using up all of the honey.
10. Sprinkle the raisins on top of the bread, covering the surface as evenly as possible.
11. In the medium mixing bowl, mix together the beaten egg, milk, vanilla, grated lemon rind, and 2 tablespoons of honey. Beat well with a large spoon.
12. Pour the milk/egg mixture over the bread.
13. Pull the shelf of your oven out part way.
14. Place the large baking pan on the shelf and place the glass baking dish or casserole into the baking pan.
15. Pour enough hot water into the large baking pan so that it is filled with 1 inch of water.
16. Gently push the oven shelf back into place and bake at 375° for 45 minutes or until the custard is done.
17. Test for doneness: When the custard seems solid at the edges and only has a small, soft spot in the center, it is done.
18. Serve bread pudding warm or hot, plain or with cream or whipped cream topping it.

Orange Date Whip

This is a no-cream whip which needs a blender. In addition to making a fine snack or dessert, it makes a great filling for cakes.

4 servings

INGREDIENTS
8 oz. pitted dates
½ cup orange juice
1 tsp. lemon juice
4 oz. shelled nuts (walnuts or pecans)

EQUIPMENT
blender
small saucepan
1 spoon for scooping out blender
measuring cup
measuring spoons
4 custard cups or dessert dishes

---

1. Simmer the dates and orange juice and lemon juice in the saucepan for about 10 minutes.
2. Pour the mixture into the blender and cover it. Blend for 30 seconds on a high speed.
3. Add the nuts to the dates and recover the blender.
4. Blend for 10 more seconds on a high speed or until the nuts are finely chopped.
5. Spoon into 4 individual serving dishes and chill. Serve cold.

Dried Fruit Cream Whip

You need a blender for this dessert. You must also begin making this whip the night before you want to eat it because the fruit must soak overnight. However, with a little planning, it is worth it because you can use your favorite dried fruit and use the resulting whip to snack on or to ice a cake or cupcakes.

6–8 servings

INGREDIENTS	EQUIPMENT
1 lb. dried fruit	3 medium mixing bowls
2 cups heavy cream	egg beater or electric mixer
honey (optional)	1 large spoon for mixing
	blender
	measuring cup

1. Soak the dried fruit in water in one of the bowls overnight. Use just enough water to cover the fruit.
2. The next day, put some of the fruit with a little of the soaking liquid into the blender. Cover and blend on high speed until it is smooth.
3. Keep adding the fruit, a little at a time and a little liquid at a time. When the blender is about ¼ full of smooth fruit, empty it into a bowl and begin again.
4. Keep repeating steps 2 and 3 until all the fruit is blended and in a mixing bowl. You may have leftover liquid.
5. In a separate bowl, whip the heavy cream until it becomes whipped cream.
6. Fold the fruit into the whipped cream with the large spoon.
7. Use as an icing on a cake or chill and serve as a snack or dessert.
8. If this whip is not sweet enough for you, add a little honey to the cream while you are whipping it.

Frozen Banana Whip

Here is a whip that can be made without a blender. It's almost like homemade banana ice cream.

4 servings

INGREDIENTS	EQUIPMENT
2 very ripe bananas	*1 fork*
½ cup honey	*2 medium mixing bowls*
½ pt. (1 cup) heavy cream	*1 large spoon for mixing*
2 tbs. lemon juice	*ice cube tray or metal bowl which*
pinch of salt	*will fit in your freezer*
	egg beater or electric mixer

1. In a mixing bowl, mash the bananas with a fork until they are smooth.
2. Add the lemon juice, honey, and pinch of salt and blend together well.
3. In the other mixing bowl, whip the cream with the egg beater or electric mixer until it is fluffy and stands in peaks.
4. Fold the banana mixture into the whipped cream.
5. Spoon the whip into an ice cube tray with the dividers removed or a metal bowl which will fit into your freezer compartment.
6. Freeze until the whip is firm but not hard. You will have to check your whip after about 20 minutes. Freezers freeze at different rates.
7. If your whip has gotten too hard, remove it from the freezer and let it stand at room temperature for a few minutes.

Apricot Whip

You must have the use of a blender to make most fruit whips. If you have one, then the possibilities for inventing new whips is endless. Try a few of the recipes in this book and then begin inventing on your own.

6 servings

Puddings, Custards, and Whips

INGREDIENTS	EQUIPMENT
1½ cups dried apricots	1 small saucepan with cover
1 cup water	blender
1 cup heavy cream	1 medium mixing bowl
½ cup honey	egg beater or electric mixer
1 thin strip of lemon peel (yellow part only)	1 large spoon for mixing
	measuring cup
	6 dessert dishes

1. In the small saucepan, mix the apricots, honey, lemon peel, and water.
2. Turn on the heat to high and bring the mixture to a boil.
3. Lower the heat as soon as the mixture boils and simmer covered for 20 minutes.
4. Remove the pan from the stove and cool the mixture completely.
5. When the mixture is cool, remove the lemon rind and pour the apricots and liquid into the blender. Cover the blender.
6. Blend on a high speed for 20 seconds or until the mixture is smooth.
7. In the mixing bowl, whip the cup of heavy cream until it turns into whipped cream.
8. Fold the apricot mixture into the whipped cream.
9. Spoon the whip into 6 dessert dishes and chill.

Frozen Berry Whip

Here is another whip-ice cream that does not need a blender. Use strawberries, blueberries, raspberries, frozen or fresh.

4 servings

INGREDIENTS

¾ cup berries, mashed

¾ cup heavy cream

¼ cup honey

1 tsp. lemon juice

pinch of salt

EQUIPMENT

1 large mixing bowl

1 ice cube tray with dividers removed or 1 metal bowl which
will fit in your freezer compartment

1 fork or potato masher for mashing berries

measuring cup

measuring spoons

egg beater or electric mixer

1. In the large mixing bowl, whip the heavy cream with the egg beater or electric mixer.
2. When the cream is whipped, fold in the honey, berries, lemon juice, and pinch of salt. Make sure the mixture is well blended.
3. Spoon the mixture into an ice cube tray or a metal bowl.
4. Freeze for one hour or until the whip is solid.
5. Remove the whip from the freezer and spoon it into a mixing bowl.
6. Beat the whip with an egg beater or electric mixer until it is fluffy.
7. Return the whip to its freezing container and freeze again for 1½ more hours or until it is solid.
8. If the final product is too frozen to spoon into dishes, let it stand for a few minutes at room temperature.
9. You can make larger batches of this frozen whip for a party a day or so in advance.

8

Fruit Concoctions

Everyone has had someone say to them, "Why don't you have a piece of fruit instead of that cookie (or candy or piece of cake)?!" I remember opening my lunch bag at school on many occasions and finding an apple or banana instead of the hoped-for cupcake or other sweet. After failing to make a trade, I would munch away on my piece of fruit, paying very little attention to its flavor and paying much attention to the cake and cupcakes being eaten by my friends.

Actually, had I taken the time to look at, smell, and taste the fruit I was eating, I would have realized that my fruit was not only beautiful but was as sweet and delicious as the sugar-filled prepackaged sweets being eaten by my friends.

We all know that fruit is good for us—but doesn't it get boring? Not necessarily. You can concoct fancy, delicious fruit treats in your kitchen that will equal any cake. Many of the desserts in this section can be packed in plastic containers and taken to school as desserts or snacks. They are fine party foods as well, especially when topped with interesting whips. The nicest thing about fruit concoctions is that your imagination can run free. Use your favorite fruits and berries, add your favorite nuts or dried fruit to them, experiment with different flavors of honey and different spices.

Once you get started, you may find that you've invented a number of fruit concoctions of your own.

Fresh Fruit

Be sure to wash all fresh fruit well before using it in a fruit concoction. Growers use insecticides and some even use spray preservatives before they ship their fruit to market. Berries can be placed in a sieve and held under cold water for a few minutes to clean them.

A Warning about Canned Fruit

If you live in an area where fresh fruit is difficult to get—especially during winter—use canned or frozen fruit. However, be warned. Read the labels on the cans to see if the fruit was packed in sugar syrup or in its natural juices. Fruit packed in sugar syrup defeats the purpose of your trying to make yourself healthy snacks. Fruit packed in natural juices is sweet, delicious, and nutritious.

Unless there is a medical reason for your eating dietetic food, also avoid dietetic fruit in cans. Most of it has been sweetened with chemicals that are not particularly good for you.

Frozen Fruit

Many companies now freeze berries so that they will be available in winter. Again, check to see if the berries have been packed in sugar or in their natural juices.

Frozen berries can be used in pies, cakes, and muffins as well as in fruit concoctions. The difference is that when defrosted, they will be soggy and swimming in their own juices (a result of the freezing process). All this means is that if you use them for baking, take into account the liquid portion of the frozen fruit when measuring out your liquid ingredients. Don't discard the fruit liquid because it contains much flavor and many vitamins and minerals. Use it as a substitute for part of the milk or water in the recipe.

Dried Fruit

There are two kinds of dried fruit available in stores. The first kind is found in most groceries and supermarkets and is dried with the aid of some chemicals. The second is the kind of dried fruit found in most health food stores; it is supposed to be dried naturally, without chemicals.

If you can't get the health food variety of dried fruit, don't worry especially since it has been discovered recently that many health food stores sell the regular commercial variety of dried fruit—they simply repackage it.

Fruit Compote

Fruit compote is fruit cooked in a syrup until it is soft. The recipe here has some of my favorite fruit in it. You can either use my suggestions or make your compote out of your favorite fruit.

4 servings

INGREDIENTS
2 peaches, sliced thin
2 apples, sliced thin

EQUIPMENT
1 large saucepan
1 large knife

INGREDIENTS

½ cup raisins

1 pear, sliced thin

1 cup honey

1 cup water

1 stick of cinnamon

2 cloves

EQUIPMENT

cutting board

1 large spoon for mixing

measuring cup

1 large bowl

---

1. Put all of the ingredients into the saucepan. Stir well. (Do not peel the fruit. Slice it with the skin.)
2. Simmer over a low flame until the fruit is just tender.
3. Remove from the heat and cool. Place the fruit and syrup in the bowl.
4. Refrigerate until ready to eat. Remove cinnamon stick and cloves before serving.
5. Serve plain or topped with whipped cream, yoghurt, or sour cream.

FOR CRISPER FRUIT

1. In a small saucepan, simmer the honey, water, cinnamon, and cloves for 20 minutes.
2. Place uncooked fruit in a large bowl.
3. Remove cloves and cinnamon from the honey/water syrup and pour the syrup over the fruit. Mix well and refrigerate.

Dried Fruit in Apple Juice

Pick your favorite dried fruit or fruits for this snack—figs, apples, apricots, pears—and make enough for second helpings. Fruit in apple juice must be made at least 24 hours before you are planning to eat it.

INGREDIENTS	EQUIPMENT
1 cup unsweetened apple juice	1 small saucepan
1 package (11 or 12 oz.) dried fruit	1 medium bowl with a cover
2 tbs. raisins	1 spoon
½ cup water	measuring cup
	measuring spoons

1. In the saucepan, mix together the apple juice and the water.
2. Bring the juice/water mixture to a boil over a high flame and immediately turn off the heat.
3. Put the fruit in the bowl.
4. Pour the apple juice/water mixture over the fruit.
5. Cover the bowl and place it in the refrigerator for 24 hours.

Fruit and Special Sour Cream

This incredible special sour cream makes a wonderful topping for almost any kind of fruit or berries. The recipe makes one cup of topping which should serve four people or two very hungry snackers. **4 servings**

INGREDIENTS	EQUIPMENT
½ pt. sour cream	1 small mixing bowl
1 tbs. honey	egg beater or electric mixer
¼ tsp. grated lemon rind	1 spoon
pinch of cloves	grater
pinch of cinnamon	measuring spoons

1. Place the egg beater or blades from your mixer and the mixing bowl in the refrigerator for about 10 minutes to chill them.
2. When they are chilled, pour sour cream into the mixing bowl and beat it until it is thick (about 5 to 8 minutes).
3. Add the honey, lemon rind, cloves, and cinnamon and blend together well.
4. Serve on top of almost any fresh fruit or berries (slice the fruit first, of course) or on top of the fruit compote or the fruit in honey.

Poached Cherries

This fruit concoction makes a wonderful snack or dessert or a great topping for ice cream or a lovely garnish for cakes.

4 servings

INGREDIENTS	EQUIPMENT
1 to 1½ lbs. red cherries	1 medium saucepan
½ cup honey	1 paring knife
1 cup water	measuring cup
pinch of salt	

1. Wash the cherries and remove their stems and pits. You do this by cutting each cherry in half with the paring knife.
2. Put the honey, water, and salt into the saucepan. Bring it to a boil.
3. As soon as it has boiled, turn down the heat to low and add the cherries.
4. Simmer the cherries in the syrup until they are tender, not mushy.
5. Serve warm or cold.

Fruit and Honey

Fresh fruit soaked in honey is a wonderful dessert or snack, especially for the warmer months of the year. Pick your favorite fruit or fruits and concoct this treat.

INGREDIENTS	EQUIPMENT
1 peach or pear or apple per person	1 large knife
or	1 bowl large enough for the fruit
½ cup berries per person	measuring spoons
2 tbs. honey per fruit or half cup of berries	measuring cup
	1 large spoon

1. Wash the fruit and slice it into thin slices, skin and all. Discard the pits or seeds.
2. With berries, wash them and pick out any stems (or cut off the stems of strawberries).
3. Put the sliced fruit in the bowl, mix in the honey and let it stand for at least ½ hour before eating.
4. Serve plain or top with ice cream, whipped cream, a favorite whip, the Special Sour Cream (p. 102), or yoghurt.

Applesauce and Apple Butter

Applesauce is a wonderful snack by itself but it also enhances a number of other snacks. It can be used to fill a cake, on top of gingerbread, or whipped with whipped cream and frozen to make apple ice cream. Apple butter is a wonderful spread for sandwiches, muffins, or homemade bread.

INGREDIENTS	EQUIPMENT
4 cups peeled and cored apples, thinly sliced	1 paring knife
	1 large knife for slicing

INGREDIENTS

1 cup water

1 tsp. lemon juice

½ tsp. cinnamon

¼ tsp. ground ginger

¼ tsp. ground cloves

⅛ tsp. nutmeg

¼ cup honey

EQUIPMENT

1 large saucepan

1 large spoon for mixing

measuring cup

measuring spoons

1 large bowl

1. Put the apple slices, water, and lemon juice into the large saucepan. Bring to a boil over high heat.
2. Turn down the heat and add the rest of the ingredients. Stir well.
3. Simmer the mixture over low heat until the apples are soft and mushy.
4. Remove from heat, mash, and stir very well with the large spoon and pour into a large bowl.
5. Refrigerate until ready to serve.

FOR APPLE BUTTER

1. Double the recipe because apple butter is really condensed.
2. Instead of removing the pot from the heat when the apples are mushy and soft, keep cooking the mixture over a very low flame until it is *very* thick. Stir occasionally.
3. Cool and store in covered containers in the refrigerator.

Baked Pears or Baked Apples

Eating a piece of fruit instead of a piece of cake or pie is no trouble at all if it is one of these baked apples or pears.

4 servings

INGREDIENTS	EQUIPMENT
4 pears or apples	1 paring knife
¾ cup honey	1 glass baking dish or 4 oven-proof
¾ cup water	custard cups
4 cloves	1 large spoon for mixing
cinnamon	1 small saucepan
	measuring cup

1. Preheat oven to 350° F.
2. Wash the fruit very well.
3. Core the apples but leave the pears whole.
4. In the small saucepan, mix the honey and water and cook it over a low flame for 3 minutes.
5. Place the fruit in a small glass baking dish or in 4 individual oven-proof custard cups.

6. Stick a clove into each piece of fruit.
7. Sprinkle some cinnamon on each piece of fruit.
8. Pour some of the honey and water mixture over each piece of fruit. Use all of the mixture.

9. Bake for 20 to 30 minutes in the 350° oven or until the fruit is tender, *not mushy*. Baste the fruit frequently with the honey/water syrup while it is baking (using a small spoon if you are baking the fruit in custard cups).
10. Serve the baked fruit cold or hot—plain or heaped with whipped cream, special sour cream, or plain heavy cream.

VARIATIONS If you want to make your baked apples very special, fill the centers of the apples with chopped dates, whole raisins or currants, chopped dried fruit, or bits of cheddar cheese before baking.

Broiled Grapefruit

These recipes are for grapefruit lovers as well as for those who may not have really loved this tangy fruit before. Try them both—I think that they will surprise you.

4 servings

INGREDIENTS	EQUIPMENT
2 grapefruits	grapefruit or paring knife
⅛ cup unsweetened coconut, shredded	scissors
	2 small spoons
2 tbs. honey	2 small dishes
1 tbs. chopped or ground nuts	measuring spoons
½ tsp. cinnamon	1 large knife

1. Turn on your oven to broil.
2. Cut the grapefruits in half.
3. Cut around the edge of the grapefruits and in between the sections to loosen them. Use a grapefruit knife or a paring knife for this operation.
4. Clip out the center core in each grapefruit half with the scissors.
5. In one small dish, combine the coconut and one tablespoon of honey. Blend well with a spoon.
6. In the other small dish, combine the chopped or ground nuts, the cinnamon, and one tablespoon of honey.
7. Spread the honey/coconut mixture on two of the grapefruit halves.
8. Spread the honey/nut/cinnamon mixture on the other two halves.
9. Place all of them under the broiler for 5 minutes or until they are lightly browned.
10. Serve warm.

Baked or Broiled Bananas

Here is a banana snack that takes only 20 minutes to make. If you like bananas, you'll love this sweet.

4 servings

INGREDIENTS

4 bananas

4 tbs. butter or margarine

4 tbs. honey

2 tsp. lemon or lime juice

EQUIPMENT

1 baking pan big enough to fit the bananas

1 sharp knife

1 small dish

1 pastry brush

1 fork

---

1. Preheat oven to 350° F. if you are baking your bananas. Turn it to broil if you are broiling them.
2. Peel the bananas and cut them in half lengthwise.
3. Grease the baking pan.
4. Arrange the bananas in the pan with the uncut side up.
5. In the small dish, blend together the lemon or lime juice with the honey using the fork to beat the mixture slightly.
6. Brush the bananas with the honey/lime or lemon juice mixture.
7. Dot the bananas with the butter or margarine.
8. *Bake:* 10 minutes at 350° or until tender but not mushy. *Broil:* Under broiler for about 10 minutes or until lightly browned.
9. Serve hot—with or without a topping. You can top these bananas with the Special Sour Cream, Whipped Cream, a favorite whip, or even ice cream.

9

Sandwiches

The sandwich, which is the most popular lunch food in the United States, is beginning to grow in popularity in other countries. It's a convenient, easy way to make and eat a meal or a snack and there is no end to the variety of food you can put between two pieces of bread or in the center of a roll.

The invention of the sandwich is credited to an English politician, John Montagu, the 4th Earl of Sandwich (a part of England). He was a gambler and invented the sandwich so that he could eat informally without leaving the gaming tables. He also served as the first lord of the admiralty several times and is said to be responsible for the decay of the British navy because he used it for his own political goals. Under his rule, ships literally fell to pieces and naval stores were sold by naval officials for personal profit. It is said that Sandwich's mismanagement of the navy contributed greatly to the British failure in the American Revolution.

Perhaps that is one reason why the food named after him gained such quick popularity in the United States.

Naturally Sweet Fruit Jam

Most jams and jellies are made with a great deal of sugar or with artificial sweeteners. Here is a jam you can easily make yourself and store in tight-fitting lidded containers in the refrigerator. There are two sets of directions—one if you have a blender or food grinder and one if you don't.

INGREDIENTS	EQUIPMENT
1 cup pitted prunes	blender or food grinder
2 cups dried figs	1 cutting board
1 cup dried apricots	1 large, sharp knife
1 cup raisins	1 large saucepan with lid
1 cup pitted dates	plastic or glass containers with lids
1 orange	measuring cup
1 lemon	heavy spoon
2½ cups water	grater
	1 large mixing bowl

Blender instructions:
1. Slice the orange and lemon into very thin slices *with the peel.* Discard the seeds and place the slices in the saucepan.
2. Place the rest of the fruit in the saucepan and add the water.
3. Cover the saucepan and simmer over a very low heat until all of the water is absorbed.
4. Turn off heat and cool.
5. When the fruit is cool, either put it through a food grinder or place it in a blender, about a cup at a time. Blend on high speed for about 1 minute. Remove the fruit from the blender and do another batch until all the fruit has been blended.

6. Mix it together very well in the mixing bowl and put it in the lidded containers for storage in the refrigerator.

No-Blender Instructions:
1. Grate the orange and lemon peels and put the gratings in the saucepan.
2. Cut up the orange and lemon into tiny pieces, discard the seeds and put the orange and lemon pieces in the saucepan.
3. Cut the rest of the fruit into tiny, tiny pieces and put them in the saucepan with the water. Cover the pan.
4. Simmer over a very low heat until all of the water is absorbed.
5. Let the jam cool and then dump it in the mixing bowl.
6. Mash it with the heavy spoon as best you can and mix well.
7. Store it in the lidded containers in the refrigerator.

Make Your Own Mayonnaise

Homemade mayonnaise is a bit more yellow and a great deal more flavorful than the store-bought kind. In addition, it is free of chemical preservatives. Store it in a tightly lidded jar in the refrigerator.   **About 2 cups**

INGREDIENTS	EQUIPMENT
2 egg yolks (and one whole egg in the shell)	*egg beater, wire whisk, or electric mixer*
1 pt. olive oil	*1 large mixing bowl*
1 tsp. salt	*lidded jar for storage*
½ tsp. dry mustard	*measuring spoons*
lemon juice or wine vinegar	

ALL INGREDIENTS MUST BE ROOM TEMPERATURE

1. With the whisk, egg beater, or electric mixer, beat the egg yolks, salt, and mustard together.
2. Begin adding the oil, *a few drops at a time*, beating the mixture thoroughly after you add every few drops.
3. If your mayonnaise begins to curdle, it means that you have been adding the oil too fast.
4. The way you correct this problem is to separate your reserve egg and in a separate bowl, beat the reserve egg yolk and slowly add a few drops of oil to it. Beat it well.
5. Gradually add the reserve beaten egg yolk and oil to your original mixture, beating it slowly.
6. Continue adding oil until your mixture is very thick and stiff. REMEMBER TO ADD THIS OIL A FEW DROPS AT A TIME.
7. Add a very small amount of vinegar or lemon juice (depending upon what you like) to thin out the mixture. Beat it in and taste. Add a little more until the taste and thickness pleases you.
8. Store in a jar in the refrigerator.

Egg Salad

Here is a spicy way to prepare an egg salad sandwich. Spread it on some homemade bread and you have a filling and healthy lunch or snack. **4 servings**

INGREDIENTS	EQUIPMENT
4 eggs	1 large sharp knife
1 ½ tsp. salt	1 chopping board
2 tbs. lemon juice	1 medium saucepan
1 tsp. Worcestershire sauce (optional)	1 fork
	1 medium mixing bowl

INGREDIENTS

½ tsp. ground red pepper (or black pepper if you don't have red)

⅓ cup mayonnaise

1 slice of onion, finely chopped

2 stalks of celery, finely chopped

¼ cup diced green pepper

EQUIPMENT

measuring cup

measuring spoons

1 large spoon for mixing

---

1. Fill the saucepan ½ full of water, put it over a high heat on the stove, and let the water boil.
2. Lower the eggs into the boiling water with a spoon and let them boil for ten minutes.
3. Remove the pan from the stove, hold it under the faucet in the sink, and let cold water run into it. When the eggs are cool enough to handle, place them in the refrigerator for at least 20 minutes and then peel them.
4. When the eggs are peeled, mash them with a fork in the mixing bowl. Keep mashing until both the yolk and the white of the eggs are in tiny pieces.
5. Add all of the other ingredients to the mashed eggs and stir with the large spoon until all ingredients are well mixed.
6. The egg salad is now ready to eat.

Toasts

Here are some suggestions for quick toast snacks. In all cases, toast your bread first.

Cinnamon and honey toast: Spread some honey on a piece of toast and sprinkle on some ground cinnamon.
Peanut butter and nut toast: Spread peanut butter on your toast and sprinkle on some chopped nuts.

Peanut butter and raisin toast: Spread peanut butter on your toast and sprinkle it with raisins.

Peanut butter and banana toast: Spread some peanut butter on your toast and cover it with sliced banana.

Honey and banana toast: Spread some honey on the toast and cover it with sliced banana.

Use your imagination. Try combinations that appeal to you even though you've never heard of them before.

Dried Apricot, Peach, or Apple Preserves

These preserves are a bit more gooey than the fruit jam. Choose the flavor you like best—apricot, peach, or apple, and try this recipe. Store the results in tightly lidded containers in the refrigerator. **About 3 cups**

INGREDIENTS

1 11 oz. package dried apricots, peaches, or apples

1 lemon

2 cups honey

2 cups cold water

¼ cup raisins

EQUIPMENT

2 medium mixing bowls

1 large saucepan with lid

1 large knife

chopping board

1 paring knife

1 small saucepan

sieve

measuring cup

---

1. Chop the apricots, peaches, or apples into tiny pieces.
2. Place the chopped apricots and the raisins in the mixing bowl with the 2 cups of cold water. Soak for 2 to 3 hours.
3. After the fruit has soaked for several hours, hold the sieve over the other mixing bowl and drain the liquid

from the fruit. Save the liquid. Place the fruit back into its own bowl.

4. With the paring knife, peel the thin layer of yellow skin off the lemon.
5. Place this peel in the small saucepan and put just enough water in the pan to cover the lemon peel. Simmer for 10 minutes and then drain off the water into the sink.
6. Cut the lemon in half and squeeze the juice from it into the large saucepan.
7. Place the drained lemon peel in the large saucepan.
8. Add 1 cup of the juice you have saved from the soaked fruit to the saucepan.
9. Add the honey and stir.
10. Simmer over a medium heat until the mixture forms a thick syrup.
11. Add the fruit to the syrup and simmer until the fruit is very soft and almost transparent.
12. Store in lidded containers in the refrigerator.

Raisin-Coconut-Yoghurt Sandwich

Here is a sweet sandwich spread that makes an ideal snack.

About 3–4 sandwiches

INGREDIENTS

½ cup plain yoghurt

½ cup unsweetened shredded coconut

½ cup raisins

EQUIPMENT

1 medium mixing bowl

1 large spoon for mixing

measuring cup

---

1. Mix all of the ingredients together in the bowl.
2. Spread on toast or bread.

Apple Butter Spread

For the recipe describing how to make apple butter, look up applesauce in chapter 8, p. 104.

Fried Banana Sandwich

Fried bananas are eaten wherever bananas are grown. Use very firm, slightly green bananas for this sandwich and treat yourself to a new taste.

INGREDIENTS	EQUIPMENT
1 firm, slightly green banana per person	spatula
1 tbs. butter or margarine per panful	1 small knife
	1 large frying pan

1. Peel the banana and slice it on an angle into pieces that are about ½ inch thick.
2. Melt the butter or margarine in the pan over a low flame.
3. Put the banana pieces in the pan and fry them until they are lightly browned, turning occasionally with the spatula.
4. Serve them warm between two slices of bread—plain or spread with cream cheese, sour cream, honey, jam, or any combination of the preceding ingredients.

Hamburger Surprise Sandwich

A hamburger is a hamburger but not always. Try this slightly different way of cooking a burger and see if you don't agree.   **4 servings**

INGREDIENTS	EQUIPMENT
1 lb. lean chopped meat	1 large mixing bowl
4 slices of tomato	1 large, heavy frying pan or char-
4 thin slices of onion	coal grill
4 slices of cheddar cheese	spatula
salt	1 large, sharp knife
pepper	

1. Put the chopped meat into the large bowl and with your hands, mix in some salt and pepper. How much depends upon your taste.
2. Place a slice of tomato, a slice of onion, and a slice of cheese on top of each other.
3. Form your hamburger patty around the cheese, tomato, and onion using ¼ of the meat. Make the hamburger a nice, round shape and be sure none of the filling ingredients show.
4. Make three more hamburgers with the cheese, tomato, and onion inside of them.
5. Before cooking, pat the hamburgers between your hands to make sure that the meat is firmly around the filling.
6. Cook on an outdoor charcoal grill or on top of the stove in a heavy frying pan. Turn several times with a spatula during cooking.
7. Make them rare, medium, or well done. However you cook these burger surprises, the cheese will be melted inside of them.
8. Serve on homemade rolls or bread instead of the standard packaged hamburger rolls.

10

Something About Flours and Oils

Flours

The kind of flour you use when you bake will effect the
final result you achieve in three ways. First of all flour will
determine the texture of your cakes, breads, pies, muffins,
and cookies; some flours produce a light, airy result and
some produce a chewy, moist baked good. Second, flour
can change the taste of a baked product. A bread or roll
baked with rye flour will taste very different from one baked
with corn flour—even if all other ingredients are the same.
Third, your choice of flour will help to determine the nutritional value of your end product; some flours have many
more vitamins and minerals than others.

It is the aim of this chapter to help you understand
enough about flour to make an intelligent choice in your
baking.

WHAT IS FLOUR?　All flours are the finely ground berries of special grasses (such as wheat, rye, and corn) or beans (such as soy). In addition to the popular flours used in the United States, there are flours made from buckwheat, barley, millet, potatoes, peanuts, and rice. Most of these can be found in health food stores or, in the case of rice flour, in oriental food stores. What people use for flour depends upon growing conditions in their part of the world.

Since the most common flour used in this part of the world is wheat flour, it will be used here to explain the nature of flour to you. Every wheat berry (just like all flour berries) has three layers—the bran, the germ, and the endosperm.

THE BRAN: This tough outer layer is rich in many vitamins, minerals and plant proteins. It protects the embryo (seed or sprout) of the plant and helps to feed it when it is becoming a new plant.

THE GERM: This is the embryo of the wheat berry (the sprout that can become a new plant). It is one of our best sources of vitamin E. The germ is also rich in the B vitamins, proteins, oil, and lecithin (a substance which is said to help our bodies use up cholesterol).

THE ENDOSPERM: This inner layer of the wheat berry is mostly starch. It has very little protein, vitamins, or minerals in it. It is used by the plant embryo (germ) as additional food during growth.

THE DIFFERENCES BETWEEN FLOURS

WHITE FLOUR: White flour is the ground endosperm of the wheat berry. In removing the bran and the germ to make white flour, food processors also remove about sixteen to twenty-eight vitamins and minerals.

White flour was originally the flour of the rich. It took many more steps to produce and the result was a much finer texture than whole grain flour. Because it was the flour of very privileged people and because of its fine texture, it was much desired by the general population. It also has the ability to last much longer than other flours without spoiling (6–8 months in an airtight container) . As refining methods were perfected, white flour took the place of whole grain flours and like other processed foods, has come to replace them almost entirely.

WHITE ENRICHED FLOUR: This is white flour which has had approximately four vitamins returned to it.

BLEACHED WHITE FLOUR: In order for a cake, cupcake, roll, or bread to be pure white after baking, some white flour is bleached. This is done by forcing gas through the flour; this gas insures that the white color will last during the baking process. Unfortunately, bleaching also removes any final trace of vitamins and minerals in the flour. Laboratory experiments with rats have shown that they will die of malnutrition if fed on a diet made up of only white bread.

UNBLEACHED (WHITE) FLOUR: This is plain white flour minus the bleaching process. When you use unbleached flour, your final product will be light brown or tan instead of pure white. It will also have no bleaching chemicals in it.

WHOLE-WHEAT FLOUR: Whole-wheat flour is flour made from the whole-wheat berry. It has all of the vitamins and minerals of the wheat berry in it. Whole-wheat flour tends to produce a chewier, heavier baked good which sometimes (depending upon how finely it is ground and whether or not you sift it) will also have some crunchy particles of the bran in it.

Always store your whole-wheat flour in a tightly sealed container in the refrigerator. It will keep for several months if this container is really airtight. If you detect a sour smell in whole-wheat flour when you are shopping, then don't buy it. If the flour smells bad (sour) when liquid is added to it, throw it out; it has spoiled.

WHOLE-WHEAT PASTRY FLOUR: Whole-wheat pastry flour is the ground whole-wheat berry from a different variety of wheat. It is more finely ground than regular whole-wheat flour and usually does not make good breads because it does not rise quite as well. Use it mostly for cookies, pie pastries, or in combination with other flours. Store it in the same way as regular whole-wheat flour.

WHEAT GERM FLOUR: Wheat germ flour is unbleached white flour with wheat germ added to it. It can be quite expensive to buy so it is suggested here that if you want to add wheat germ to your flour, do it yourself. This is a good thing to do if you are baking bread and can't find whole-wheat flour in your local stores. Buy a jar of wheat germ (usually found near the dry cereals) and add from ½ cup to 1 cup to the flour in the recipe. You'll be adding both flavor and nutrition to your cooking.

GLUTEN FLOUR: Gluten is the protein portion of the wheat berry. Gluten in flour makes dough elastic and allows you to knead it or roll it. It also holds the yeast, baking powder, or baking soda bubbles so that a baking product will rise well. Gluten flour is a special flour with extra gluten in it. It is about 50 percent protein and is low in starch. Usually it is used for special diets (such as for diabetics) or is added to other flours in commercial baked goods.

RYE FLOUR: Rye flour is flour made from whole rye berries. It has very little gluten in it so it produces a rather heavy, chewy and tasty bread. It is not used to make cakes, cookies, or pies; rye flour is, however, often mixed with other flours when making breads or rolls.

CORN MEAL AND CORN FLOUR: Both corn meal and corn flour are made from the ground corn kernels (or berries). Corn meal is coarser than corn flour which is very finely ground. Read the labels on the packages before buying corn meal or flour because some have been "degerminated." This means that the germ of the corn kernel was removed before grinding and the flour or meal lacks most of the vitamins and minerals. There are several excellent whole corn meal and flour products; they are available in markets and health food stores in most parts of the country.

SOY FLOUR OR POWDER: Soy flour is flour made from the ground soy bean. It is very high in protein and is usually added to other flours in small quantities (a tablespoon or two) to enrich the final product. If you are using unbleached white flour, add a tablespoon or two of soy flour to your batter or dough for some extra nutrition.

STONE GROUND FLOURS: These are flours ground by slow-moving stone mills. They are often favored by people interested in health food because the slow moving grinding stones give off less heat than the high speed mills used in most commercial flour processing plants. Since heat destroys some of the vitamins and minerals in the flour, stone ground flours tend to be a little richer in nutritional value.

SOME ADVICE ABOUT SIFTING FLOUR

When you sift stone-ground, whole-wheat flour, you will find a number of pieces of the crunchy brand left in your sifter. If you are making a chewy, course bread, dump these into the bowl and use them. If you are making a cake or light rolls or a pie crust, save these bran particles, store them in a tightly sealed jar in the refrigerator and use them at a later time in a bread pudding, cereal, or bread recipe.

IF YOU CAN'T FIND WHOLE GRAIN FLOUR

It is not always possible to buy whole grain flours in your neighborhood or town. It is also true that some breads and fancy cakes don't do well when you use whole grain flour—they come out too coarse and chewy. In fact, some of the recipes in this book will suggest that you use plain unbleached flour.

Two ways to enrich baked goods made with unbleached white flour have been suggested to you: add wheat germ to the breads and/or soy flour to the breads, pies, cakes and cookies. You will also be using honey, molasses, fruit, nuts, milk, yoghurt, and eggs in the baked snacks in this book so the nutritional value of your cooking will be enhanced in many ways. However, if you cannot get whole wheat flour at all, be sure to get the necessary vitamins and minerals it supplies from eating some whole grain cereals occasionally.

Oils

All people need some fat and oil in their diets. Our bodies make essential fatty acids from the fats and oils we eat, they use fats and oils for needed energy, and some essential vitamins are dissolved in fats and oils.

In cooking, we use fats and oils for four purposes.

1. They add richness and flavor to cooking (for example, butter or margarine in vegetables or oil in salad dressings).
2. We use fats and oils to fry or sauté food.
3. Fats or oils are needed to shorten (tenderize) baked goods such as pies, breads, cakes, and biscuits.
4. Fats and oils are needed to grease baking pans so that

the baked product can be removed easily when it is done.

Chapter one discussed the two kinds of oils and fats we eat—saturated and unsaturated. Saturated fats include all animal fats and some specially processed vegetable oils. Unsaturated fats and oils consist of most vegetable oils sold in stores.

Since it is believed that the eating of too much saturated fat causes a build-up of cholesterol in our bodies, it is recommended here that you use mostly unsaturated fats and oils in your cooking. Your body will get all of the saturated fat it needs in meat, whole milk, butter, margarine, eggs, and ice cream.

Here is some information about some of the oils and cooking fats you will find in food stores.

MARGARINE: Margarine is made from vegetable oils which are naturally unsaturated. However, in order to make these oils solid, the oils are put through a chemical process called hydrogenation (they are filled with hydrogen molecules). This process turns the unsaturated oils into a saturated end product. However, a number of foods cook better with margarine (such as pie crusts) so use it when you are cooking but in moderation.

SHORTENINGS: Solid shortenings such as canned shortenings and lard have been chemically treated so that they don't even need refrigeration. They are more saturated than margarine and have many chemicals in them. Try to avoid their use.

VEGETABLE AND NUT OILS: There are many vegetable and nut oils which come from the crushed seeds of a number of plants. These unsaturated oils not only add flavor to your cooking but are easy to use. They are easily mixed in with other ingredients and do not have to be creamed (softened) or melted.

You can find corn, soy, safflower, cottonseed, peanut, corn germ, and many other vegetable oils on the shelves of your local markets and health food stores. Read the labels on the bottles of oils and try to find one that is pure—without chemicals or preservatives in it. Any oil which has been processed without chemicals should be stored in the refrigerator once opened.

COLD PRESSED OILS: Most health food stores and some supermarkets sell cold pressed oils. These are more expensive vegetable oils which have been produced in presses rather than in high speed grinding mills. Cold pressed oils are richer in vitamin E because normal pressing procedures destroy most of the vitamin E.

Cold pressed oils usually have a layer of soft particles on the bottom of the bottle. These particles are simply part of the seed which have not been strained out of the oil. They are rich in vitamins and minerals and will not effect your cooking. Shake the bottle well before using the oil so that you get the full benefit of the seed particles.

IF YOU CAN'T FIND COLD PRESSED OILS   Don't worry if you can't find or can't afford the special cold pressed oils. Find another oil with a flavor that pleases you and use it. The recipes in this book often make suggestions as to the kind of oil to use but most of the suggestions are my personal taste. If you can't find a specific oil, by all means substitute.

A WARNING   Olive oil is a vegetable oil with an extremely strong flavor. Don't use it for baking. It is best used for salad making and for frying certain foods.

General Baking Rules

When you hear someone say, "I can cook but I can't bake," they are usually talking about making cakes, cookies, and pies. The reason they say this is that they don't know about certain rules which must be followed when baking sweets.

The first rule regarding good results in baking is do not experiment with changing ingredients until you are an expert. Small changes in certain ingredients in cake, cookie, and pastry recipes mean possible disaster. For example, a cake minus half the required baking powder or soda will not rise properly; a cake with twice the amount of baking powder or soda than is called for will rise too much and become dry. If you add ½ cup of extra liquid to a cake batter, you will get a very soggy cake. Leave out ½ the necessary shortening in a pastry crust and you might find that you can't bite into it after it is baked.

The solution is easy. If you read the following rules and follow them carefully, you will be able to turn out delicious baked sweets.

1. Read the entire recipe before beginning. Make sure that you have all of the ingredients that are needed. If you don't understand some of the cooking terms used in the recipe, look them up.
2. Preheating: Turn on your oven before you begin mixing the ingredients. An oven should heat-up at least 20 minutes before a baked sweet goes into it.

    Since many ovens do not have accurate thermostats, get yourself an oven thermometer (under $2.00) and put it in the oven. Check the temperature after about 15 minutes. You may find that if you set the heat at 350° F., the actual oven temperature is 400°. If that is the case, turn down the temperature a bit and re-check it in 10 minutes. (My oven is very old and so hot that I must keep the door propped open a tiny bit in order to bake.)
3. Place all of the bowls, pans, spoons, and ingredients you will need on a table or counter before you begin to mix together ingredients. Make sure they are within easy reach.
4. Make sure that you have the proper size baking pans before beginning a recipe. If you use a giant pan for a small amount of cake batter, you will wind up with a very large flat cookie and not a cake. Also, if you bake a cake for the stated amount of time in a pan that is much too large, it will be overcooked or even burnt. If you bake it in a pan that is much too small, it will be underdone. The baking pan or pans you use do not have to be the exact size stated in the recipe—but they should be close to it.
5. Check to see if all of your food ingredients are fresh. Year-old baking powder or soda that has been standing around open will not make a cake rise as it should. Flour which has been left open in an unsealed con-

tainer will have absorbed a great deal of moisture and will cause cakes, cookies, and pie crusts to be soggy. Such flour will probably also be spoiled.

6. Try to use *unsalted* margarine or butter for cakes, cookies, and pastries. If you absolutely cannot get unsalted margarine or butter, *do not* add additional salt to the batter—even if the recipe calls for salt. In addition, cooking oils and other shortening will work in cakes, cookies, and pie crusts but not quite as well as margarine and butter.

7. Read your recipe again. Make sure you understand all of the steps in it. Recheck your ingredients. Make sure they are all there.

8. Greasing or oiling baking pans: Unless the recipe tells you not to, all pie pans, cake pans, and cookie sheets should be greased or oiled before the batter or dough is placed in them. In the case of pies and cakes, grease or oil both the sides and the bottom of the pan. Always set aside a little extra butter, margarine, or cooking oil for this job.

9. Dusting: When baking cakes, it is a good idea to dust the inside of the pan with flour after you grease or oil the pan. Put a little flour into the pan, move the pan around so that the flour coats the bottom and sides and then turn the pan upside down and dump out any extra flour.

10. Measurements: Remember to use only standardized measuring tools and level measurements (see chapter 2 and 3). If the recipe calls for sifting flour before measuring, then do it. It will make a big difference in the results.

11. Premeasure all of your spices and liquid ingredients (and any nuts, fruit, and so forth). Set them aside in small dishes within easy reach. This will insure that

you do not forget to add something and will prevent you from adding something twice. This will also give you the opportunity to soak anything that needs to be soaked (for example, raisins).

12. Eggs: Always use eggs at room temperature. Take them out of the refrigerator at least one hour before using them. If the recipe calls for separate egg whites and yolks, separate them as soon as you remove them from the refrigerator (see illustration, p. 32).

13. Doubling or Halving the Recipe: If you want to make half of a recipe or if you want to make twice the amount in the recipe (doubling it), do the necessary math *before* you begin to mix ingredients. Work out the amounts of *every* ingredient and write them down. If you forget to include all of the ingredients in your figuring, you will get a strange result. For example, half the amount of flour combined with the regular amount of honey will give you a sickly sweet, sticky mess.

14. Where to Place Cakes, Cookies, and Pies in the Oven: Most ovens have at least two movable racks. If you are baking two layers of a cake and cannot fit them on the same shelf, try to put the two racks as close to the center of the oven as possible—leaving enough room between them for the cakes to rise. The same rule applies for pies and cookie sheets only you don't have to worry about rising during baking.

Heat rises so the hottest part of your oven is near the top. If you put baking products too near the top of the oven, the top of your cake, pie or cookies will get overdone and the middle and bottom of your cakes and pies will be undercooked. If you place a baked product too near the bottom of the oven, the heat coming from the electric coils or gas fire will overcook the bottom of it.

If necessary (if your oven is very small), bake things separately (one layer or pie or cookie sheet at a time). The extra time it takes will be justified by the results you get.

15. Baking Time: Unlike measurements, baking time in recipes is only an approximate time. Each oven is different and the freshness of ingredients will effect how long something should bake. Check your cake or pie from time to time.

16. Try not to bang any doors or drop any heavy objects while a cake is baking. The rising is taking place in the oven and the shock of a loud noise (the sound waves) might make the cake "fall" or collapse in the middle.

17. Testing for Doneness: Since each oven cooks differently, you should always test your cakes and cookies for doneness a few minutes before the time stated in the recipe is up.

Cakes: Use a cake tester (a special thin, metal pick), a wooden toothpick, a wooden matchstick (not the striking end), or a dry, clean fork. Stick it into the center of the cake and if it comes out clean (almost dry), the cake is done. If it comes out with tiny pieces of soggy cake sticking to it, the cake should be returned to the oven for a few more minutes.

Cookies: Read what the cookies are supposed to look like. If the recipe says "lightly brown," don't leave them in until they are dark brown. Also, for thick cookies, you can use the toothpick test on them. For thinner cookies, gently press the top of the cookies with your finger. If it springs back quickly, it is done. If your finger leaves a dent in the cookies, they need more baking time.

Always test one cookie at the front and one at the back of the cookie sheet. Some ovens cook faster in one spot. If this is true of your oven, then remove those cookies that are done and return the rest to the oven.

18. All baked products should be cooled on a cake rack so that air can freely circulate around them (see chapter 3 for directions about making a cake rack). A cake or pie which is placed directly on a counter top to cool will not cool evenly and will not be as good as one cooled on a rack.

    Cakes, muffins, and cupcakes are always cooled in their pans and tins for at least 15 minutes before removing them.

    Pies are cooled in their tins and usually served in the tins in which they are baked.

    Cookies are removed from the cookie sheets as soon as they come out of the oven and cooled directly on the cake rack. Use a spatula to remove them.

19. To remove cakes from their baking pans: After letting your cake cool for 15 minutes in its pan on the rack, take a spatula or knife and gently separate the sides of the cake from the sides of the pan. Take the pan from the rack. Place the rack (make sure it is clean) on top of the cake and turn it quickly upside down. Hold the cake rack and cake pan together while you are doing this. Put the entire upside-down assemblage on a counter or table and gently remove the cake pan.

    If you have constructed your own cake rack, put it back on its raised supports, cake and all. Let the cake cool until it is entirely cooled off. When you can no longer feel any warmth coming from it, it is ready to frost or ice.

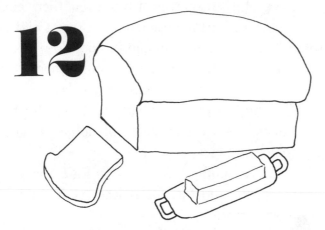

12

Breads, Rolls, Biscuits, and Crackers

If you've never baked bread before, you will be delighted to discover that it's not very difficult to do. Because bread is so readily available at supermarkets, corner groceries, and bakeries, people have stopped making it at home. In fact, people have begun thinking of bread baking as an old-fashioned, difficult, and mysterious art. They feel that it takes too much time (some breads do take a long time to prepare and some don't) and is not worth the trouble.

The truth is that you don't have to know any mysterious secrets and you don't have to have any special hidden talents to bake bread. All you must do is follow the recipes carefully and be willing to spend a little time. No bakery or supermarket bread will ever taste or smell as good as the loaf you bake yourself.

Bread making is part of the history of every living human being. Archaeologists have found hardened remains of bread baked in the Stone Age. This means that human beings have been making bread for at least 500,000 years.

Of course that early bread was quite a simple affair—not much like the fluffy bread of today. Stone Age people had nothing but stone tools to work with. They made their flour by crushing different nuts or grains between hard stones. Then they mixed this flour with water and baked it on flat or convex stones which were heated on an open fire. The top of these flat breads were covered with hot ashes which were brushed off when the bread was done. This method of baking may seem distasteful to you but even today, people who do wilderness camping sometimes use it to bake bread in the woods. The difference is that modern campers bring along ground flour and, therefore, don't have to crush their own grain.

As time went by, bread baking became more and more important to human beings. Bread was filling, nutritious, easily carried, and tasty. People invented different ways to grind grains and more and more efficient ways to bake the bread such as roasting pits, stone ovens, iron-, wood-, oil-, and coal-burning ovens and, finally, the modern gas and electric stoves and ovens you are accustomed to seeing. Modern commercial bakeries even have gigantic ovens that will bake thousands of loaves at a time.

But even before these modern ovens were invented, people had, for hundreds of years, begun using community ovens to bake bread and roast meat. It was easier in a small village to keep one oven going than to cut or dig fuel and stoke sixty or seventy ovens. Then, especially in cities, people began to offer a baking service to other people. These bread bakers opened shops which were the earliest bakeries. Over the centuries, they developed into the bakery as you know it—a place where you can buy breads, cakes, pies, and cookies of all shapes, sizes, and tastes.

However, today most people in industrialized countries don't even buy their bread at bakeries. They go to supermarkets or grocery stores and buy packaged breads which are full of chemical preservatives and taste pretty much the same.

When you bake your own bread, you will discover that each bread has its own special flavor and use, which depend upon what you put into your bread and how you cook or bake it. First there is the flour one uses. Wheat flour is the most common flour used throughout the world. The interesting thing is that there are many different kinds of wheat and many ways to process it. Each kind of wheat and process produces a special flavor and texture in a bread. You can imagine how varied the flavor of a bread can be when you consider how many different kinds of grains are used for bread making.

A few of the grains commonly used throughout the world are: rye in northern Europe, maize and corn meal in the United States (an American Indian contribution), millet in southern Europe, rice and cereal grains in India and China, buckwheat in Russia, Holland, and the United States, beans, peas, vegetable seeds and the meat of the tapioca plant in South America. Many of these grains are available in your local supermarkets and health food stores in their ground form (flour) so that you may experiment with them if you wish.

The second group of things which determines flavor are the spices or fruits or vegetables you can add to your breads. In some parts of the world, bread is eaten as a main dish at a meal and in some parts it is eaten as a dessert or a snack. You can make sweet bread or vegetable bread or simple delicious bread to eat with your meals.

The third way to change the flavor of your bread is by cooking it in different ways. A fried bread will have a very different taste and texture from a baked bread.

Breads come in all shapes and sizes. Sometimes the

shapes are simply decorative but often the shape and size of a bread has to do with its use. The long, thin Italian and French breads were originally designed so that they could be easily picked up, carried to the fields and torn or cut apart. The small, flat Indian breads (chapattis) are used as eating utensils to scoop up food. You control the shape and size of the bread you make by the way you prepare the dough and the method you use to cook it.

There are two basic ways to prepare a bread dough. The first is the old kneading method and the second is the method which requires you to mix a batter and pour it into a pan. Before you try either method, read the following directions carefully.

Kneading Dough

Many bread and roll recipes tell you to knead the dough but few explain just how to do this. It's not very difficult to do. All you must have is a little patience and some muscle power.

The only exception to this rule is if you happen to have an electric mixer with a dough hook. If you do not have this attachment, NEVER PUT DOUGH THAT CALLS FOR KNEADING INTO AN ELECTRIC MIXER WITH REGULAR MIXING BLADES OR INTO A BLENDER. If you do, you will wind up with a sticky blob of dough which is not kneaded.

To knead dough, follow these directions:

1. Sprinkle a little flour on a clean wooden cutting or dough board or on a smooth formica table or counter top.
2. Put your dough on top of the floured surface.
3. Dust your hands with a *little* flour to keep them from sticking to the dough.

4. USE THE SMALLEST AMOUNT OF FLOUR NECESSARY ON YOUR HANDS AND ON THE BOARD OR TABLE SURFACE. Too much flour will make your bread tough.
5. Push your fingers into the dough.
6. Now press down with the heels of your hands and roll the dough back and forth two or three times as you press.
7. Turn the dough one quarter of a circle.
8. Keep repeating steps 5, 6, and 7 and every time you complete a full circle, fold the dough in half so that the dough is kneaded in all directions and on all sides.
9. Keep pressing with your fingers, rolling with the heels of your hands, turning and folding the dough until it is elastic and smooth in texture (it should feel like your ear lobe) .

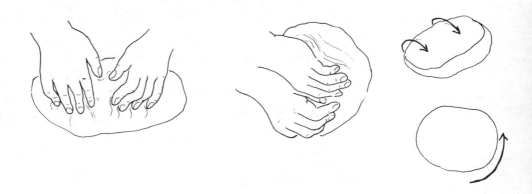

This will take longer for some breads. It all depends upon the kind of flour you use. Since no two flours are exactly alike, *you might have to add some extra flour to the recipe* if you find that after four or five minutes of kneading, the dough is sticking to your hands and to the board and is not holding together.

Rising

When cookbooks refer to bread rising, they are talking about how bread dough puffs up before or during baking. If you are making a bread out of poured batter, the rising will usually take place while the bread is in the oven. If you are making a kneaded bread however, much of the rising will take place before you bake the bread. Always check your recipe because rising out of the oven takes time. *You can't begin baking a kneaded bread one hour before you intend to eat it.*

Bread rises for several reasons. First there is a natural substance in the flour called gluten. Gluten helps make the bread rise. Some people do not add any special rising ingredients to their breads and just depend upon the natural rising action of the gluten. You may do this but if you do, you must leave the dough standing from six to twelve hours. You will find that bread made this way is very heavy, very chewy, and often hard to slice and to digest.

More common methods of making bread rise include the use of baking powder, baking soda, or yeast. Baking powder and baking soda are chemical compounds. They interact with the dough and produce carbon dioxide which makes the bread rise. The gas disappears during the baking but the bread keeps the shape it was pushed into by the gas. Both baking powder and soda are most often used in poured bread batters.

Yeast is a natural, living organism. When mixed with the dough, it releases carbon dioxide gas and makes the dough expand. In order to live and work, yeast must have warmth, air and moisture. This is why you should always keep it in the refrigerator in a sealed package until you are ready to use it. Yeast is sold in solid, moist, rectangular cakes or in packages of dry granules.

Active dry yeast (granules which come in foil packages, often premeasured in 1 tablespoon amounts) will keep for years if it is kept dry and cool. Once you wet it, however, it comes to life. It will work well when mixed with warm liquid or very hot liquid.

Cake yeast is alive and will spoil (or die) much faster than dry yeast. If you see mold on a yeast cake then it is either dead or dying—throw it out. Too much heat will kill cake yeast so always dissolve it (by mashing it up) in tepid (lukewarm) water.

If you only use part of the active dry yeast or cake yeast, be sure to wrap the remainder well (in cellophane wrap) and return it to the refrigerator.

One cake of yeast = 1 tablespoon of active dry yeast

USING YEAST

When you use yeast, always mix it with approximately ¼ to ½ cup of warm water and a few drops of honey, sugar, or juice concentrate (such as carrot or cherry concentrate). Any kind of sugar (fruit or vegetable or honey) helps the yeast to begin working. Let this mixture stand in a warm place for about five minutes or until it becomes foamy. Then add it to your dough. The only exception to this procedure is when the recipe specifically gives you other instructions.

IF YOUR YEAST WON'T BUBBLE AND OTHER PROBLEMS

If you cannot get your yeast mixture to bubble or foam, it means that the yeast is too old and will not make your bread or rolls rise. Thow it out and get new yeast.

Do not use too much extra liquid to dissolve the yeast or your dough will get sticky and soggy. In fact, if your recipe calls for any water at all, use part of it to dissolve the yeast. For example, if you need 2 cups of water for your dough, use 1½ cups for general mixing and ½ cup for your yeast mixture.

DIRECTION FOR BREAD RISING

When making a bread which requires rising out of the oven (usually the same bread requires kneading), follow these directions:

1. To rise properly, the dough must be kept at a warm temperature and out of all drafts.

2. Place the dough in a large bowl and cover it lightly with a clean, linen or lightweight towel. (Don't use a heavy bath towel or you'll squash your dough).

3. Put the bowl in a spot where the temperature is about 80° to 90° F. A good place is near a warm stove, on top of the refrigerator (the motor of a refrigerator generates heat), on top of a radiator (with a stone slab or a bunch of newspapers under the bowl), on top of a warm television or over a sink or bathtub filled with hot water (be sure that the bowl is secure and can't tip over). One other good place is in front of a sunny window but make sure that there are no drafts coming through.

4. Make sure you let the dough rise to the correct bulk. Your recipe will tell you what this is. Don't be impatient because this can take some time—an hour or more with some flours and yeasts or as little as half an hour with others. Check every twenty minutes or so the first time you try a recipe.

5. If your dough rises too little (that is, if you get impatient or if your yeast is old and weak), your bread will turn out soggy. If it rises too much (you forgot about it and left it too long), your bread will be very coarse and dry in texture.

6. Test for readiness: To see if your dough is ready, do the

following. Near the side of the bowl, gently push a finger into the dough half way to the first knuckle (about ½ inch). Wiggle the finger gently and then pull it out. If the dough stays where it is, leaving a hole, it has risen enough. If the hole slowly fills up with dough, let it rise a bit longer. Don't poke too deeply into the dough or you will ruin the rising process by breaking too many of the gas bubbles.

7. Most recipes requiring out-of-the-oven rising, tell you to let the dough rise at least two times, kneading in between risings. *Don't take shortcuts!* Don't decide to let it rise just once. Follow the recipe. If there were an easier, shorter way to bake that particular bread, the recipe would indicate it.

Doubling Recipes

If you feel that this way of making bread takes too long a time for one or two loaves, why don't you double or triple the recipe and bake a whole batch of breads. Fresh bread, after it has cooled, can be wrapped carefully (so that it is airtight) and frozen for future use. That is if it doesn't all get eaten at one sitting.

How to Tell When Your Bread Is Baked

No two ovens cook in exactly the same way; some are slightly hotter and some cooler. Altitude also affects baking time so if you live at sea level, your bread will bake faster than a bread baked by someone living on top of a mountain. Test your bread before removing it from the oven to cool.

The best way to test for doneness is to take a dry, clean knife, a clean piece of wire, or a toothpick and push it through the center of the loaf all the way to the bottom of the pan. Wiggle it a tiny bit and then pull it out carefully.

If the tool you used has soggy, lumpy dough stuck to it, put the bread back to bake for five or ten more minutes and then test it again. If the tool comes out almost clean, your bread is done.

Special Equipment Needed for Bread Baking

The only special equipment you'll need for baking bread will be loaf pans—if they are mentioned in the recipe. These are rectangular pans made out of glass, aluminum, tin, or tin foil (tin-foil pans are disposable but can be reused several times). Loaf pans can be found in different sizes which range from 7 to 10 inches long, 3 to 6 inches wide, and 2 to 2½ inches high. If the recipe calls for a large loaf pan, try to use one that is close to the 10x6x2½-inch size. If it calls for the use of small loaf pans, try to use pans close to the 7x3x2-inch size. Don't worry about being too exact with these measurements—being close to them will be fine.

If your recipe calls for a loaf pan, don't try to bake your bread in a cake pan or you will wind up with a rather flat, cake-shaped bread. However, if you absolutely cannot get a loaf pan, try shaping the loaf with your hands or, better yet, take some tin foil, bend it into the proper shape and place your dough in it. When baking, put your homemade loaf pan on a small sheet of tin foil or on a cookie sheet. Be sure if you use this homemade-loaf-pan method, that you pinch the edges so that they are secure. Remember, the last rising always takes place in the baking pan and as dough rises, it also expands. Your homemade pan must be strong enough so that the dough will not simply split it at the seams. Since this takes place before you bake it, you can always correct your mistakes if you see your tin-foil pan begin to fall apart.

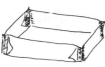

Simple Rye Nut Bread

This dark, moist bread is a delicious snack and sandwich treat. If you cannot get rye flour, then substitute whole wheat flour in the recipe. The results will still be delicious.

1 large or 2 small loaves

INGREDIENTS	EQUIPMENT
2½ cups rye flour	1 small mixing bowl
⅓ cup vegetable or nut oil	1 large mixing bowl
1 cup chopped walnuts	1 small dish for beating egg
1 cup milk	measuring spoons
1 egg slightly beaten	measuring cup
½ cup honey	1 large spoon for mixing
1½ tsp. baking powder	1 large or 2 small loaf pans
1 tsp. vanilla extract	cake rack
½ tsp. salt	

1. Preheat oven to 350° F.
2. Mix together (in a small mixing bowl) the oil and the honey.
3. Add the egg and the vanilla to the oil/honey mixture. Mix well.
4. In the large mixing bowl, mix together the flour, salt, baking powder, and the nuts.
5. Pour a little of the milk into the flour mixture. Stir.
6. Add some of the honey/oil/egg mixture to the flour mixture. Stir.
7. Keep repeating steps 5 and 6 until you have a nice, smooth mixture with all of the ingredients in one bowl.
8. Oil or grease a large loaf pan or two small loaf pans.
9. Spoon the batter into your pan or pans.

10. For a large loaf bake for 40 minutes at 350° or until done. For a small loaf bake for 25 to 30 minutes or until done.
11. Cool for a few minutes on the rack and then remove from the pan or pans.
12. Finish cooling the bread on a rack.

Raisin Bread

Raisin bread is difficult to find in stores these days. Perhaps it is just as well because this recipe produces a bread that disappears within minutes when it is put on the table. Slice it thin and eat it with honey, butter, margarine, cream cheese, or just plain. Serve it warm, cold, or toasted—any way it's delicious.

1 large or 2 small loaves

INGREDIENTS	EQUIPMENT
2½ cups whole wheat or unbleached flour	sifter or sieve
1 tsp. baking soda	2 medium mixing bowls for sifting flour
1 egg	egg beater or fork
2 tsp. cinnamon	1 large mixing bowl
½ tsp. salt	1 large spoon for mixing
¼ cup oil	1 large or 2 small loaf pans
¾ cup honey	cake rack
⅔ cup plain yoghurt	measuring spoons
¾ cup raisins, soaked in water until soft and then drained	measuring cup
¼ tsp. ground cloves	

1. Preheat oven to 350°.
2. Sift flour *twice* with baking soda, salt, cinnamon, and cloves.
3. In a separate large bowl, beat the egg until it is bubbly.
4. Add the honey and oil to the beaten egg. Stir well.
5. Add some of the yoghurt to the egg mixture. Stir well.
6. Add some of the flour to the yoghurt/egg mixture. Stir well.
7. Repeat steps 5 and 6 until all of the ingredients are in one bowl.
8. Make sure that your raisins are drained and soft. Mix them into the flour/egg/yoghurt batter. Stir very well.
9. Oil or grease 1 large or 2 small loaf pans.
10. Spoon the batter into the pan or pans.
11. Bake at 350° for one hour (for the large loaf) or for 45 minutes (for two small loaves) or until done.
12. Cool on cake rack out of the pan.

Three Easy Breads with One Basic Recipe

These breads are best when eaten hot (or warmed up) and are great at breakfast or snack time. The recipe makes two 8-inch square loaves so you can make at least two kinds of bread at one time.

INGREDIENTS	EQUIPMENT
4 cups sifted unbleached flour	1 large mixing bowl
1 cup wheat germ	1 large spoon for mixing
2 tbs. baking powder	1 small mixing bowl
2 eggs	2 8-inch square baking pans
1 cup honey	cake rack
1 cup vegetable or nut oil	sifter or sieve

INGREDIENTS	EQUIPMENT
1½ cups milk	egg beater or fork
½ tbs. salt	measuring cup
	measuring spoons

1. Preheat oven to 375° F.
2. Combine the sifted flour, wheat germ, baking powder, salt, and honey in a large mixing bowl. Mix well.
3. In the small mixing bowl, beat together the eggs and the milk until they are foamy.
4. Add the milk/egg mixture to the flour mixture and stir until you get a lumpy batter.
5. Add the oil to the flour/milk/egg mixture and stir very well until it is thoroughly mixed in.
6. Grease or oil two 8-inch square baking pans and spoon in the batter.
7. Bake in a 375° oven for 25 to 30 minutes or until brown on top.
8. Remove the breads from the pans and cool them on the cake rack.
9. If you decide to freeze these breads, wrap them so that they are air-tight. When you remove them from the freezer, do not defrost them. Simply put them into a preheated 350° oven for 10 minutes after taking them out of the freezer and unwrapping them.

CINNAMON NUT BREAD (one loaf)

INGREDIENTS

Easy Bread Basic Batter

½ cup honey

½ cup chopped nuts

1 tsp. cinnamon

After the batter is in one of the pans but *before baking,* spread the honey on top of the loaf and sprinkle it with nuts and cinnamon. Bake as directed. If you want to make both loaves into cinnamon nut bread, simply double the amount of nuts, cinnamon, and honey.

APPLE BREAD (one loaf)

INGREDIENTS
Easy Bread Basic Batter
2 cups sliced, peeled apples
½ cup honey
¼ tsp. nutmeg
¼ tsp. cinnamon

---

1. *Generously* grease (with margarine or butter) an 8-inch or 9-inch square baking pan.
2. Cover the bottom of the pan with layers of apple. Use all of the 2 cups of apples.
3. Sprinkle the apples with nutmeg and cinnamon.
4. Pour the honey over the apples.
5. Spoon one half of your Easy Bread Basic Batter over the apples, honey and spices.
6. Bake at 375° for 25 to 30 minutes.
7. Cool for a short while in the pan and then turn out onto a cake rack—apple side up.

Peanut Butter Bread

If you like peanut butter, you will love this bread. It is very delicious and easy to make. It is most delicious on the second day.

1 medium loaf

INGREDIENTS	EQUIPMENT
2 cups whole-wheat or unbleached flour	sifter or sieve
4 tsp. baking powder	1 large bowl and 1 small bowl
⅔ cup peanut butter	1 egg beater or electric mixer
¼ cup honey	1 medium loaf pan
1¼ cups milk	measuring spoons
½ tsp. salt	measuring cup
	1 large spoon for mixing
	cake rack

1. Preheat oven to 350° F.
2. Sift together flour, baking powder, and salt.
3. Add milk and honey to peanut butter and blend well.
4. Add milk/peanut butter mixture to flour mixture and beat thoroughly.
5. Oil or grease your loaf pan.
6. Spoon batter into loaf pan and bake at 350° for 40–50 minutes or until done.
7. This bread will be a little moist when done so the toothpick will come out with a few particles of sticky dough on it when you test for doneness.
8. Cool on a cake rack out of the pan.

Boston Brown Bread

There are hundreds of recipes for the slightly sweet, very filling brown bread which is eaten with baked beans and frankfurters. This recipe is a traditional steamed variety. It is delicious by itself or with cream cheese on it, and it makes wonderfully filling snacks for chilly fall or winter days.

2 loaves

INGREDIENTS	EQUIPMENT
2¼ cups whole-wheat or un-bleached flour	1 large mixing bowl
¾ cup cornmeal	1 small mixing bowl
⅔ cup raisins	1 large spoon for mixing
¼ cup honey	2 1-quart casserole dishes (oven proof) or 2 clean 1-pound coffee cans with their lids.
1 egg	
¾ cup molasses	1 large pot with steaming rack and cover
1 tsp. salt	
1½ tsp. baking powder	1 small dish for beating egg
1½ tsp. baking soda	1 egg beater or fork
1¾ cups buttermilk	1 tea kettle or saucepan
2 tbs. vegetable or nut oil	

1. In the small mixing bowl, mix together the oil and honey.
2. In the small dish, beat the egg until it is bubbly.
3. Add egg and molasses to honey/oil mixture. Beat well.
4. In the large bowl, mix together flour, cornmeal, salt, baking powder, and baking soda.
5. Add oil/honey/molasses mixture to flour. Stir in thoroughly.
6. Add buttermilk to the mixture. Beat until smooth.
7. Fold in the raisins.
8. Grease the casserole dishes or the coffee cans very well. Also grease the lids of the coffee cans (the inside surface).
9. Spoon the batter into the casserole dishes or coffee cans, filling them a little more than one half full.
10. Cover coffee cans with greased lid or tin foil. Cover 1-quart casserole dishes with foil. If you use foil, tie it down with a string.

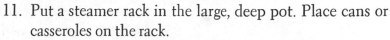

11. Put a steamer rack in the large, deep pot. Place cans or casseroles on the rack.
12. Boil water in a tea kettle or in a saucepan. Pour the boiling water into the large pot so that it comes half way up the sides of the coffee cans or casseroles.
13. Cover the pot and steam over a medium flame for about 2½ hours.
14. Remove from pot, remove the lids, and turn upside down on clean surface.
15. Serve hot or cold.

Lemon and Molasses Bread

This bread is almost a cake. It's sweet, moist, and great if you like to eat your breakfast on the run.

1 large or 2 small loaves

INGREDIENTS	EQUIPMENT
2½ cups whole wheat or unbleached flour	2 medium mixing bowls (for flour sifting)
⅔ cup yoghurt	1 large mixing bowl
1 egg	egg beater
1½ tsp. grated lemon peel	1 large spoon for mixing
1 tsp. baking soda	1 large or 2 small loaf pans
½ tsp. cinnamon	grater
½ tsp. salt	measuring cup
½ cup molasses	measuring spoons
¼ cup vegetable or nut oil	flour sifter or sieve
¼ cup honey	cake rack
1½ tbs. lemon juice	

1. Preheat oven to 350° F.
2. Sift the flour *two times* with the baking soda, salt, and spices.
3. In the large mixing bowl, beat the egg until it is bubbly.
4. Add the honey, molasses, oil, lemon juice, and lemon peel to the beaten egg. Stir well.
5. Add some of the yoghurt to the egg mixture. Stir well.
6. Add some of the flour to the egg mixture. Stir well.
7. Keep repeating steps 5 and 6 until all of your ingredients are in one bowl. Stir until the mixture is smooth.
8. Oil or grease 1 large or 2 small loaf pans.
9. Spoon the batter into the pan or pans.
10. Bake 1 large loaf for one hour. Bake 2 small loaves 40–50 minutes or until done.
11. Cool bread on cake rack.

Rice Bread in a Blender

If you don't have a blender at home, then add extra water to your rice and cook it until it is mushy. Follow all other directions except beat the ingredients where it says blend. You'll find this is a delicious bread especially when it is sliced and toasted. It should be served very fresh or re-heated before serving. If you like grilled cheese sandwich snacks, then this is the bread for them.

2 small or 1 large loaf

INGREDIENTS

1 envelope active dry yeast

1 tsp. salt

1 cup cooked rice

1½ cups warm milk

EQUIPMENT

blender

1 large mixing bowl

1 large spoon for mixing

measuring spoons

INGREDIENTS	EQUIPMENT
1 beaten egg	measuring cup
3 tsp. honey	sifter or sieve
4½ cups sifted whole wheat or un-	1 large or 2 small loaf pans
bleached flour	1 lightweight towel
½ cup lukewarm water	cake rack for cooling
	1 fork for beating egg
	pastry brush

1. Preheat oven to 375° F.
2. Into your blender container, put the yeast, 1 tsp. of honey and the lukewarm water.
3. Let it stand for 5 minutes and then cover and blend on the high speed for 20 seconds.
4. Turn off the blender and add to the container the milk, 2 tsp. of honey and the cooked rice.
5. Cover the container and blend again on high for 10 seconds.
6. Put the sifted flour in a large mixing bowl.
7. Pour the yeast, honey, rice, milk mixture over the flour.
8. Stir with a large spoon until the dough is well mixed.
9. Oil or grease a large pan or 2 small loaf pans.
10. Dust your hands with flour and shape the dough into 1 or 2 loaves so that it or they will fit into your pan (or pans) .
11. Cover the loaf (or loaves) with a clean, lightweight towel and let the dough rise until it is double in bulk.
12. Brush the top of the breads with the beaten egg.
13. Bake in the 375° F. oven for 50 to 60 minutes or until nicely brown.
14. Test the loaves for doneness.
15. If done, cool on the rack *in the loaf pans.* Remove the bread after it is thoroughly cool.

Banana Bread with Yoghurt

For a spicy, sweet breakfast, snack, or party treat, try this bread. It's great with cream cheese, butter, margarine, jam, or just plain.

1 large or 2 small loaves

INGREDIENTS

2 large, ripe, mashed bananas

3 cups whole wheat or unbleached
   flour

2 eggs

1 cup honey

1 tsp. baking soda

½ tsp. baking powder

½ cup plain yoghurt

½ tsp. salt

½ cup vegetable or nut oil

½ tsp. cinnamon

¼ tsp. ground ginger

EQUIPMENT

1 small mixing bowl

1 medium mixing bowl

1 large mixing bowl

sifter or sieve

1 large spoon for mixing

1 large or 2 small loaf pans

measuring spoons

measuring cup

cake rack

1. Preheat oven to 350° F.
2. In a small bowl, mix together the yoghurt and mashed bananas.
3. In a medium mixing bowl, sift together the flour, salt, cinnamon, baking powder, baking soda, and ginger.
4. In a large bowl, mix together the honey, oil, and 2 eggs.
5. Add a little of the yoghurt and banana mixture to the honey and oil mixture. Stir well.
6. Add a little of the flour mixture to the yoghurt/banana/honey/oil mixture. Stir well.
7. Keep repeating steps 5 and 6 until all ingredients are in one bowl.

8. Mix very well until smooth.
9. Oil or grease one large or two small loaf pans.
10. Spoon your batter into the pan or pans.
11. For a single large loaf, bake 1 hour or until done. For 2 small loaves, bake 45–55 minutes or until done.
12. Cool for a few minutes and then remove from pan or pans.
13. Cool bread on a cake rack.

Fruit and Nut Bread

Fruit and nut bread is about as close to a cake as a bread can get. It is a marvelous snack treat or breakfast food. If you like it enough, you can even ice it and serve it as a dessert or at a party.

1 medium loaf

INGREDIENTS	EQUIPMENT
3 cups unbleached flour	2 medium mixing bowls
¼ cup honey	1 large spoon for mixing
½ tsp. salt	1 medium loaf pan
1 cup chopped nuts	measuring cup
1 cup mixed chopped dried fruit	measuring spoons
1 egg, well beaten	cake rack
4 tsp. baking powder	1 large knife for chopping fruit
grated rind of one lemon	grater
¾ cup evaporated milk (6 fluid oz.)	
2 tbs. vegetable or nut oil	
½ cup water	

1. Preheat oven to 350° F.
2. Mix the flour, honey, salt, and baking powder in a medium-sized mixing bowl.
3. Add the nuts and fruit to this mixture and stir in well.
4. In a separate bowl, mix all of the remaining ingredients.
5. Slowly add the mixture of milk/egg/oil to the flour mixture. Stir very well.
6. Grease or oil the medium loaf pan.
7. Spoon the batter into the loaf pan.
8. Bake for 60–65 minutes or until done.
9. Remove the bread from the oven and let it stand for about ten minutes in its pan on the rack.
10. Remove from the pan and let it cool on the rack.
11. This bread should be wrapped in foil or cellophane paper and stored in the refrigerator. It will keep about one week this way.

Pumpkin Bread

Yes, Pumpkin Bread. You can buy a can of pumpkin at your supermarket or grocery store. If you use canned pumpkin, *be sure to buy pure pumpkin* and *not* pumpkin pie filling which is full of sugar, preservatives, and flavoring. If you use fresh pumpkin, look at the recipe in the pie section for cooking a pumpkin (p. 239).

2 small loaves

INGREDIENTS	EQUIPMENT
3 cups whole-wheat or unbleached flour	1 large mixing bowl
1½ cups mashed cooked pumpkin	1 large spoon for mixing
2 tbs. vegetable or nut oil	1 clean, lightweight towel
	2 small loaf pans

INGREDIENTS

2 tbs. warm water

1 yeast cake (or 1 tbs. active dry
   yeast)

¼ tsp. salt

1 tsp. cinnamon

1 tsp. nutmeg

½ cup honey

½ cup chopped nuts

¼ tsp. ground cloves

EQUIPMENT

measuring cup

measuring spoons

cake rack

1. In a large mixing bowl, dissolve the yeast in the warm water with a few drops of honey. Let it stand until it is foamy.
2. Add the oil, salt, spices, pumpkin, honey, nuts, and enough of the flour (about one cup) to make a smooth mixture.
3. Cover the bowl with the lightweight towel and let it stand in a warm place until the mixture is light and airy.
4. When the mixture is light and airy, add the remaining flour and mix very well.
5. Cover the bowl again and let the dough rise until it is double in bulk.
6. Oil or grease two small loaf pans.
7. Divide the dough in half and place it in the loaf pans. Shape the tops of the breads gently so they are nice and round.
8. Preheat your oven to 350° F.
9. Let the dough rise until the centers of the loaves are a little above the edges of the pans.
10. Bake at 350° for 40 minutes or until done.
11. Cool on a cake rack out of the pans.

Hom Yoke Bow (Chinese Filled Rolls)

A popular Chinese luncheon dish and snack, Hom Yoke Bow are always a treat. These filled rolls are, in fact, eaten all over the Orient and have as many names as there are fillings to go in them. You can fill them with almost anything sweet or make them into a satisfying meal by filling them with just about any kind of cooked meat.

12–14 rolls

INGREDIENTS	EQUIPMENT
1 cake of yeast (or 1 tbs. active dry yeast)	1 large bowl
	1 small bowl
1 cup warm water	1 lightweight towel
2 cups unbleached white flour	cookie sheet or large baking pan
1 tbs. vegetable or nut oil	1 small saucepan
	pastry brush

1. In the small bowl, dissolve the yeast in the warm water and set aside until it is foamy.
2. Put the flour in the large bowl.
3. Make a hole in the center of the flour and pour the yeast/water mixture into it.
4. Using your hands, squeeze and mix the flour and yeast until you get a dough.
5. Turn the dough out onto a floured surface and knead it until it is the texture of an earlobe. (See step 6 before finishing kneading.)
6. While you are kneading, add the oil and knead it in.
7. Place the dough in a large, clean bowl and cover it with a clean, *damp* lightweight towel. Set it in a warm place.
8. Let the dough rise until it is 3 *or* 4 times its original size. Approximately 1½ to 2 hours.

Breads, Rolls, Biscuits, and Crackers

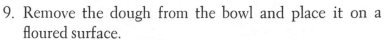

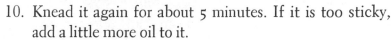

9. Remove the dough from the bowl and place it on a floured surface.
10. Knead it again for about 5 minutes. If it is too sticky, add a little more oil to it.
11. Divide the dough into 12 to 14 equal parts and roll each part into a ball with your hands.
12. Make a hole in each ball with your finger.
13. Put some stuffing into each hole and close up the hole by pinching the dough around it.
14. Roll each dough ball between your hands again so that they are round.
15. Put the rolls in a warm place for 30–40 minutes or until they rise to double their original size.
16. Preheat your oven to 350° F.
17. In a small saucepan, melt some butter or margarine (about 1 tbs.) and some honey (about 2 tbs.). Stir well.

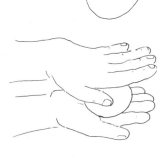

18. Brush the top of each roll with the melted mixture and place the rolls on a greased cookie sheet or in a greased large baking pan.
19. Bake for about 20 minutes or until they are golden brown on top.

FOR STEAMING: Instead of baking the rolls, they can be steamed. Follow directions 1 through 15. Then proceed as follows:

16. Fill a steaming pot (or large kettle) with several inches of water.
17. Place a steaming rack in the pot.
18. After the rolls have risen to double their bulk, place them on the rack and steam them (cover the pot) for about 15 or 20 minutes.

In both cases, steaming and baking, Hom Yoke Bow are best served warm. You can make them beforehand and re-heat them for eating.

Breads, Rolls, Biscuits, and Crackers

Sweet fillings:
You can really let your imagination go wild here. You can fill your bow with chopped dates, chopped figs, jelly, jam, crushed pineapple, apple sauce, raisins, crushed beans (such as Chinese bean paste which can be bought in a Chinese grocery), or anything sweet that will stand some cooking.

Meat fillings:
Make tiny meatballs out of chopped meat and spices. Cook them on top of the stove in a frying pan or in the oven and stuff them into the rolls. Or chop up some cooked sausage or leftover chicken, fish, or ham or stuff them with sardines. Again—use your imagination and experiment. Make several different kinds of Hom Yoke Bow at once.

Basic Roll Recipe

There is as much difference between freshly baked home-made rolls and heat-and-serve rolls as there is between a sixteen-cent hamburger and a six-dollar steak. This recipe makes 24 rolls and the leftovers (if there are any) can be wrapped carefully and frozen for future eating.

INGREDIENTS	EQUIPMENT
3 cups sifted whole-wheat or un-bleached flour	1 egg beater or electric mixer
1 cup lukewarm water	1 large mixing bowl
1 tbs. active dry yeast (or 1 yeast cake)	1 lightweight towel
	2 muffin tins (with 12 cups in each)
1 egg	1 large spoon for mixing

1 egg yolk slightly beaten
1 tsp. salt
¼ cup vegetable or nut oil
a few drops of honey

1 pastry brush (see Chapter 3, p. 36, for substitution)
measuring cup
measuring spoons
sifter or sieve
cake rack

---

1. Mix the yeast, water, and a few drops of honey in a large mixing bowl. Let it stand for 5 minutes or until it is foamy.
2. Add the oil, 1 egg, and salt to the yeast mixture.
3. Beat with a hand beater, electric mixer, or vigorously with a spoon for 1 minute.
4. Add the flour to the yeast/egg/oil mixture. Mix it thoroughly with the large spoon.
5. Cover the bowl with a lightweight towel and set it in a warm place. Let the dough rise until it is double in bulk (about 1½ hours).
6. After it has risen, stir the dough with a large spoon so that it collapses.
7. Oil or grease the muffin tins well.
8. With a spoon, fill each cup in the muffin tin half full of dough. Set it aside in a warm place.
9. Preheat your oven to 375° F.
10. Let the rolls rise until they are double in bulk (about 30–45 minutes).
11. Brush the top of each roll with a little beaten egg yolk.
12. Bake at 375° for 25 minutes or until lightly browned on top.
13. Cool on a rack out of the tins.

FLAVORED ROLLS

1. You can top the rolls with poppy seeds or sesame seeds before baking.
2. You can make sweet rolls by putting some honey and chopped nuts on top of each roll before baking.

BASIC ROLLS MADE FANCY

The nice thing about basic recipes is that you can change them quite easily and make something really special to snack on. Try some of the following suggestions with your basic roll recipe.

24 rolls

INGREDIENTS

(for 4 flavors—6 rolls each)

Basic Roll Recipe

¼ cup drained, crushed, canned pineapple

¼ cup raisins, soaked until soft, and drained

¼ cup finely chopped walnuts mixed with 2 tsp. cinnamon and 2 tsp. honey

¼ cup grated hard cheese (such as cheddar)

EQUIPMENT

4 small bowls

4 small dishes

grater

All equipment listed under Basic Roll Recipe

4 spoons

1. After the Basic Roll Recipe has risen (step 5), stir it down and divide it into 4 equal parts.
2. Place each portion of dough in a small bowl and add one of the 4 flavors listed above to each.

3. Stir each mixture well (using a clean spoon for each) .
4. Fill your oiled muffin tins ½ full.
5. Let the rolls rise for 45 minutes or until they are double in bulk.
6. Bake in a preheated oven at 375° F. for 25 minutes or until lightly brown on top.
7. Cool on a rack out of the tins.

All of these roll recipes can be served warm or cold.

Basic Biscuit Dough

Biscuits are usually smaller and flakier than rolls. They are wonderful snack treats especially when spread with honey or peanut butter. They are also great at a party when served with something hot like chili. A special party treat for your friends would be tiny grilled-cheese open sandwiches made on homemade biscuits.

INGREDIENTS	EQUIPMENT
2 cups unbleached flour	1 large bowl
¾ cup milk (approximately)	1 rolling pin (optional)
2 tsp. honey	1 knife
1 tsp. salt	sifter or sieve
5 tbs. vegetable or nut oil or mar- garine	measuring cup
2½ tsp. baking powder	measuring spoons
2 tsp. soy powder or flour (op- tional)	cookie sheet or large baking pan

1. Preheat oven to 450° F.
2. Sift all of the dry ingredients into the large mixing bowl.
3. Add the honey and the oil to the dry ingredients.
4. Gently work in the honey and the oil with your fingertips.
5. Pour in some of the milk.
6. Again, work in the milk with your fingers.
7. Keep repeating steps 5 and 6 until you get a smooth, soft dough that is not too sticky to be handled.
8. You may not use up all of the milk.
9. Lightly flour a clean surface.
10. Turn the dough out of the bowl onto this surface.

For square biscuits:
11. Pat the dough with your hands or roll it very gently with a lightly floured rolling pin. For fluffy biscuits, roll it or pat it until it is ½ inch thick. For crunchy biscuits, roll or pat it until it is ¼ inch thick.
12. Cut the dough into strips which are 1 inch wide.
13. Cut each 1-inch strip into pieces that are 1½ inch long.
14. Oil or grease your cookie sheet or baking pan.
15. Place the biscuits on the sheet or in the pan and bake at 450° for 12 to 15 minutes or until they are lightly browned.

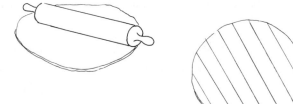

For round biscuits:
Instead of cutting the dough into strips, take a cookie cutter or a clean glass and cut the dough into circles.

For cheese biscuits:
Add about ⅓ cup grated cheese (cheddar, swiss) to the dough during step 3.

For raisin-nut biscuits:
Add ½ cup of soaked and drained raisins and ½ cup of finely chopped nuts to the dough during step 3.

Crackers

Homemade crackers are so crisp, fresh tasting, and easy to make that you may never buy packaged crackers again. Eat them with soups, spread with peanut butter and jelly, or with dips at parties. Add a little honey to the recipe, sprinkle them with cinnamon before baking and you have a very simple cookie. There is no way of telling how many crackers a cracker recipe makes because it depends upon how thin you roll the dough.

INGREDIENTS	EQUIPMENT
1 cup whole-wheat or unbleached flour	1 medium mixing bowl
¼ tsp. salt	rolling pin
2 tbs. softened margarine or butter	cookie sheet or large baking pan
⅛ tsp. baking powder	measuring cup
water (cold)	measuring spoons
	sifter or sieve
	cake rack

1. Preheat oven to 350° F.
2. Sift flour, salt and baking powder into the mixing bowl.
3. Add the margarine or butter and work it in with your fingers.
4. Add just enough water to make a nice, not too sticky, dough. If you add a little too much and find that your dough is too gooey, just add a bit more flour.
5. Place the dough on a lightly floured surface.
6. Knead the dough until it has the texture of an earlobe.
7. Scrape any extra dough off the clean surface.
8. Sprinkle a little more flour on the surface and roll out the dough with a lightly floured rolling pin as thin as possible.
9. Cut the dough into 2-inch squares.
10. Grease a cookie sheet or a large baking pan.
11. Place the crackers on the sheet or the pan.
12. Bake at 350° until your crackers are crisp and brown.
13. Remove crackers from sheet or pan and cool on a cake rack.

If you like flavored crackers, divide the dough and knead a favorite flavor into each portion such as: garlic powder, grated cheese, onion powder, sesame seeds. Use your imagination and be inventive.

Sesame Seed Crackers—Fried or Baked

Sesame seed crackers are so good and versatile that you can spread almost any kind of food on them for a delicious snack. They add to the flavor of practically anything—from peanut butter to tuna fish or clam dip.

INGREDIENTS	EQUIPMENT
2 cups buckwheat, whole-wheat, or unbleached flour	spatula
	1 large mixing bowl

INGREDIENTS

1 *cup ice water*

5 *tbs. softened margarine or butter*

½ *tsp. salt*

½ *cup sesame seeds (lightly roasted)**

¼ *tsp. baking powder*

vegetable or nut oil (for fried crackers)

EQUIPMENT

1 large, sharp knife

1 heavy skillet (frying pan) or 1 cookie sheet (for baking)

paper towels (for frying) or cake rack (for baking)

---

1. In a large mixing bowl, mix all of the ingredients together.
2. Using your hands, gently squeeze and mix the dough until you get a stiff, pastelike dough. If it is too sticky, add a little more flour.
3. Lightly flour a board, table top, or clean counter.
4. Put the dough on the board and roll it with your hands into the shape of a fat sausage.
5. Using a large knife, cut very thin slices from the sausage-shaped dough.
6. Flatten the slices to a thickness you like with the palm of your hand (remember these are crackers) .

Fried Crackers:

1. Heat up a heavy, large skillet with 2 tbs. of oil.
2. Put several crackers in the skillet and turn them often with a spatula until both sides of each cracker are crisp and brown.
3. Remove these from the pan with the spatula and drain them on paper towels.
4. Keep repeating the frying process, adding extra oil when necessary, until all of your crackers are cooked.

* Put the sesame seeds in a heavy skillet *without* any oil. Over a high flame, cook them while stirring constantly until they are golden, light brown.

Baked Crackers:
1. Preheat your oven to 350° F.
2. Place the crackers on a greased cookie sheet.
3. Bake until the crackers are brown and crisp, 12 to 15 minutes.

Chapattis (East Indian Bread)

Chapattis are eaten in India with curries and other foods that are easily scooped up onto this flat bread. You can make them to eat with curry or chili or you can serve them at parties with dips. Chapattis are also a great crunchy snack for television-watching or studying.

10 chapattis

INGREDIENTS	EQUIPMENT
1 cup sifted whole-wheat flour	1 large bowl
⅛ tsp. salt	sifter or sieve
½ cup water	1 clean lightweight towel
a pinch of curry powder, a pinch of chili powder, and a pinch of freshly ground pepper (optional)	1 rolling pin
	waxed paper
	1 heavy skillet (frying pan)
	spatula

1. Sift flour and salt (and curry, chili, and pepper if you like hot food) into a large bowl.
2. Using your fingers to mix, slowly add just enough water to make a soft dough.
3. Divide the dough into 10 pieces.
4. Flatten all of the pieces into circles (using the palm of your hand) on a lightly floured surface.
5. Cover with a lightweight towel and let the dough stand for 20 minutes.

Breads, Rolls, Biscuits, and Crackers

6. After the 20 minutes are up, roll out each chapattis with a rolling pin. Roll them out as thin as possible. If you have waxed paper, put the dough circle between two large sheets of it and then roll. When the chapattis is almost paper thin, peel off the waxed paper and set the chapattis aside and roll another. If you don't have waxed paper, sprinkle a little flour on the dough before you begin rolling it.

7. *For crisp chapattis*, put about 1 tbs. of oil in a heavy skillet or on a flat griddle. *For softer chapattis*, cook without oil. In both cases, heat the skillet for 2 or 3 minutes over a high flame then turn the flame down a bit.

8. Put as many chapattis as will fit in the skillet without overlapping.

9. With a spatula, turn them frequently until both sides of each bread are light brown. Chapattis puff up a bit as they cook.

10. If you are using oil, add more for the second batch if it has been used up.

11. To keep flat, press down with spatula while cooking.

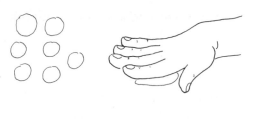

Breads, Rolls, Biscuits, and Crackers

13

Cupcakes and Muffins

Cupcakes and muffins are grouped together here because they are usually baked in the same way. The difference between the two is that cupcakes are miniature cakes which are often made with icing and filling. Muffins are usually not as sweet, are often eaten hot with a meal (breakfast or lunch usually), and do not have icing on them. Muffins are, therefore, more like a sweet, miniature bread and are often eaten with jellies, jams, margarine, or butter spread on them.

To make most muffins or cupcakes, you need a muffin tin so that each small cake or bread can bake in its own container. Many people buy special small paper containers which fit inside the muffin tin. The batter is poured directly into these containers and the cake or bread is baked in them. Each finished product then lifts easily out of the muffin tin and is encased in its own paper "jacket." These paper containers are not necessary for you to use but sometimes make the eating of the final product neater and less crumbly. If you intend to pack your cupcakes or muffins in your lunch bag or box, paper jackets might be a good idea for you to consider.

Cake Recipes and Cupcakes

Any cake recipe can be used to make cupcakes. Just remember to cut the baking time down to at least half of what the cake recipe calls for. If you don't, you will wind up with a number of charcoal cakes. Check the cupcakes frequently to see how they are doing. They bake very fast.

Testing for Doneness

To see if your cupcakes or muffins are done, take a dry toothpick and push it through the middle of several of the cupcakes or muffins until it touches the bottom of the tin. Pull it out. If it is dry or almost dry, they are done. If it comes up with soggy, doughy bits sticking to it, put the tin back for a few minutes. Be sure to test at least one cupcake or muffin in the front and in the back of the muffin tin. Some ovens have cooler areas. If you find that some are done and some aren't and feel that 3 or 4 more minutes in the oven will burn those that are ready, you will have to remove them carefully, ignoring the directions below. However, this does not happen very often so don't worry about it.

Cooling Cupcakes and Muffins

Cupcakes and muffins should be cooled on a cake rack. Muffins are delicious served warm so you don't have to cool them thoroughly. However, cupcakes should be absolutely cool before you ice them.

Removing Cupcakes and Muffins from the Tin

If you have not used paper "jackets," in order to remove cupcakes and muffins from their tins, do the following:

1. Let the entire tin cool down for about 5 minutes.
2. Take a clean, dry knife and slide it between the edge of each cupcake or muffin and the tin.
3. Making sure that the knife is touching the bottom of the tin, slide it around the entire muffin or cupcake.
4. Do this to all of the muffins or cupcakes.
5. Turn the muffin tin upside down over a clean surface or gently lift each muffin or cupcake out.
6. If any are stuck to the bottom of the tin, gently try to ease your most flexible knife (usually a grapefruit knife) under the cupcake or muffin. Then turn the tin upside down and tap the bottom of the stuck cupcake or muffin.
7. Place all of the freed cupcakes and muffins on the cake rack to cool.
8. If you oil or grease the muffin tins very well before pouring in batter, you will not have a sticking problem.

Regular Old Cupcakes

There are times when you will want to eat a plain cupcake that has no fancy taste other than some old-fashioned sweet goodness. The nice thing about plain cupcakes is that you can make them into miniature layer cakes by cutting each one in half and adding filling to it. You can then make a sandwich of the two halves and ice the outside. If you like raisins, then consider adding ½ cup of presoaked and drained raisins to the batter before spooning the batter into the muffin tins.

12 cupcakes

INGREDIENTS	EQUIPMENT
1 cup sifted unbleached white flour	sifter or sieve
¾ cup honey	2 medium mixing bowls
½ cup milk	1 heavy spoon (for creaming)
¼ cup butter or margarine (room temperature)	egg beater or electric mixer
	1 large spoon for mixing
¼ tsp. salt	1 muffin tin (with 12 cups)
1 tsp. baking powder	cake rack
1 egg	measuring cup
½ tsp. vanilla extract	measuring spoons

1. Preheat oven to 375° F.
2. Sift together the flour, salt, and baking powder.
3. In a separate bowl, cream the shortening and honey.
4. When the shortening and honey are creamed together, beat the mixture with the egg beater until it is light and fluffy.
5. Add the egg to the shortening/honey mixture and beat well.
6. Add a little flour to this mixture and beat well.
7. Add a little milk to the mixture and beat well.
8. Keep repeating steps 6 and 7 until all of the flour mixture and milk are combined with the shortening/honey mixture.
9. Stir in the vanilla so that it is thoroughly mixed in.
10. Grease or oil your muffin tin (or line each cup with a paper jacket).
11. Spoon the batter into the muffin tin cups.
12. Bake at 375° for 20 minutes or until done.
13. Cool on a cake rack.

Fruit Cupcakes

These incredibly filling, spicy cupcakes are practically a meal. Ice them with your favorite icing or leave them plain. Either way they will provide you with a snack pick-up that is difficult to surpass.

About 16 cupcakes

INGREDIENTS

½ cup raisins

½ cup chopped dates

½ cup chopped figs

½ cup chopped prunes

¼ cup chopped walnuts

⅔ cup honey

¼ cup milk

1¼ cups whole-wheat or un-bleached flour

¼ cup vegetable or nut oil

1 tsp. baking powder

1½ tsp. baking soda

¼ tsp. cinnamon

⅛ tsp. salt

¼ tsp. ground cloves

⅛ tsp. ground nutmeg

pinch of ground ginger

1 cup water

EQUIPMENT

1 medium saucepan

sifter or sieve

1 large mixing bowl

1 large mixing spoon

cake rack

1 medium mixing bowl

1 muffin tin with 12 cups

measuring spoons

measuring cup

1. Preheat oven to 350° F.
2. Put water and dried fruit into saucepan with all of the spices and boil until the fruit is tender. Remove from stove and cool a little.

3. Sift the flour *two times* with the baking power, baking soda, and salt so that it winds up in the large mixing bowl.
4. Add the honey to the flour and mix well.
5. Add the milk, oil, fruit, and the liquid the fruit cooked in to the flour/honey mixture and stir well.
6. Stir in the nuts and mix very well.
7. Oil or grease the muffin tin very well (or line 12 muffin cups with paper jackets).
8. Spoon into the muffin tin.
9. Bake for 30 minutes at 350° F. or until done.
10. Cool on rack.

Carob Cupcakes

Chocolate flavor without chocolate—that's what you'll get when you make these carob cupcakes. This recipe makes 12 cupcakes.

INGREDIENTS	EQUIPMENT
1 cup sifted unbleached flour	1 muffin tin with 12 cups
½ cup buttermilk (or ¼ cup milk and ¼ cup sour cream)	1 large mixing bowl
	1 medium mixing bowl
¼ cup carob powder	egg beater or electric mixer
4 tbs. butter or margarine	1 large spoon for mixing
½ tsp. baking soda	measuring cup
½ tsp. vanilla extract	measuring spoons
2 eggs	sifter or sieve
½ tsp. salt	1 heavy spoon for creaming
	cake rack

1. Preheat oven to 350° F.
2. Sift the flour, salt, baking soda, and carob powder into the medium-sized mixing bowl.
3. In the large mixing bowl, cream the butter or margarine until it is smooth.
4. Add the eggs to the creamed shortening and beat very well until the mixture is fluffy.
5. Add the flour mixture to the shortening/egg mixture and mix well.
6. Add half the milk and the vanilla to the flour/shortening/egg mixture and beat well. (If you are using regular milk and sour cream instead of buttermilk, add the milk at this point.)
7. Add the rest of the milk (or the sour cream) to the batter and beat well.
8. Grease the muffin tin and dust each cup lightly with flour (or line each muffin cup with paper jackets).
9. Spoon the batter into the muffin tin cups so that each cup is about ¾ full.
10. Bake for 25 minutes or until done.
11. If you have leftover batter, make a second batch of cupcakes when the first batch is baked.
12. Cool on a rack and ice.

Peanut Butter Raisin Cupcakes

These cupcakes are especially delicious when iced with a whipped cream icing that has had a few tablespoons of peanut butter beaten into it. This recipe is for 8 cupcakes so if your muffin tin has 12 cups in it, *do not* try to fill them all up with batter. Leave four of them empty.

INGREDIENTS

½ cup whole-wheat flour

EQUIPMENT

2 medium-sized mixing bowls

INGREDIENTS

¼ cup unbleached white flour (or
   ¾ cup unbleached flour)
1 tbs. wheat germ (optional)
¼ tsp. salt
½ tsp. baking soda
3 tbs. peanut butter
1 tbs. vegetable or nut oil
½ cup raisins
1 tbs. molasses
1 egg
½ cup milk
⅓ cup honey
⅛ tsp. cinnamon
boiling water

EQUIPMENT

2 table knives
1 small bowl for soaking raisins
muffin tin
measuring cup
measuring spoon
1 large spoon for mixing
strainer (sieve)
fork
cake rack
small pan for boiling water

1. Preheat oven to 375° F.
2. In a medium-sized mixing bowl, combine the flour, wheat germ, salt, cinnamon, and baking soda.
3. Cut the peanut butter into the flour mixture with two knives.
4. Add the oil and honey to the flour/peanut butter mixture. Stir.
5. Put the raisins in a small bowl and pour some boiling water over them. Soak them for 3 minutes. Pour the raisins and water into a strainer over the sink and shake the strainer until the raisins are fully drained.
6. Add the raisins to the flour/peanut butter/honey mixture. Stir well.
7. In a separate bowl, combine the molasses, egg, and milk, and beat with a fork until the 3 ingredients are well mixed.
8. Add the molasses/egg/milk mixture to the flour mix-

ture and stir until all ingredients are well mixed.

9. Oil or grease 8 muffin cups in your muffin tin or place 8 paper jackets into 8 of the cups.
10. Spoon the batter into these 8 cups.
11. Bake at 375° F. for about 25 minutes or until done.
12. Cool on a cake rack.
13. Remember to cool the cupcakes thoroughly before icing them.

Banana Cupcakes

These banana cupcakes are a triple treat. First of all they have the delicate flavor of banana in them. Second, they have a filling which is baked into them and third you can ice them with your favorite icing. Served at a gathering of friends, they are sure to bring you many compliments.

8–12 cupcakes

INGREDIENTS

1 cup unbleached flour

¼ cup butter or margarine (room temperature)

1 egg

1 tsp. baking powder

½ tsp. baking soda

½ tsp. salt

½ cup mashed ripe banana

2 tbs. milk

½ tsp. vanilla extract

⅔ cup honey

jam, jelly, applesauce, fruit compote, or chopped nuts

EQUIPMENT

1 large mixing bowl

2 medium mixing bowls

1 heavy spoon for creaming

1 egg beater or electric mixer

1 muffin tin with 12 cups

1 large mixing spoon

measuring cup

measuring spoons

cake rack

---

1. Preheat oven to 375° F.
2. In a large mixing bowl, cream the butter or margarine and honey.
3. Add the egg to the creamed mixture and beat well.
4. In a medium-sized mixing bowl, mix together the flour, salt, baking powder, and baking soda.
5. In the other medium mixing bowl, combine the mashed banana, vanilla, and milk. Mix well.
6. Add some of the flour mixture to the creamed mixture and stir well.
7. Add some of the banana/milk mixture to the creamed mixture. Stir well.
8. Keep repeating steps 6 and 7 until all of the ingredients are in one bowl. Mix very well.
9. Grease or oil your muffin cups (or line them with paper jackets).
10. Drop one heaping tablespoon of batter into each of the muffin cups.
11. Then drop ½ tsp. of jam, jelly, applesauce, fruit compote, or chopped nuts into each muffin cup.
12. When each muffin cup has some filling and batter in it, drop another heaping tablespoon of batter into each cup, covering the filling.
13. Bake for 20 to 25 minutes in a 375° oven or until done.
14. Cool on a rack and ice. Try a cream cheese icing or, for a powerful banana flavor, a banana icing.

Applesauce Muffins

These chewy muffins have an applesauce surprise in the center. Serve them plain, warm or cold; or spread with butter, margarine, jam, or jelly. They are a nice change from bland store-bought muffins.

12 muffins

INGREDIENTS

2 cups whole-wheat or unbleached
  flour
1 egg
1 cup milk
4 tbs. vegetable or nut oil
1 heaping tbs. baking powder
2 tbs. honey
1¼ cups thick applesauce

EQUIPMENT

1 muffin tin with 12 cups
1 fork for beating egg
1 large spoon for mixing
1 small bowl
2 medium mixing bowls
1 large mixing bowl
measuring spoons
measuring cup
sifter or sieve
cake rack

1. Preheat oven to 350° F.
2. In the small bowl, beat the egg with a fork until it is bubbly.
3. In a medium mixing bowl, mix together the oil, milk, and honey.
4. Sift the flour *two times* with the baking powder and salt so that it winds up in the large mixing bowl.
5. Add the oil/milk/honey mixture to the flour mixture. Stir well.
6. Add the egg to the batter and mix all ingredients together lightly. Do not beat.
7. Oil or grease the muffin tins or line them with paper jackets.
8. Put one level tablespoon of batter into each muffin cup.
9. Put one heaping tablespoon of applesauce into each muffin cup over the batter.
10. Fill the muffin cups to the top with batter.
11. Bake for 30 minutes or until done at 350°.
12. Cool on a rack.

Cupcakes and Muffins

Corn Muffins

Corn muffins come in boxed mixes, frozen, wrapped in cellophane, and, most often, stale or soggy. Once you taste your own made-from-scratch recipe, you'll never want another packaged or premixed imitation.

12 muffins

INGREDIENTS	EQUIPMENT
1¼ cups corn meal	1 medium mixing bowl
¾ cup unbleached flour	1 large mixing bowl
3 tbs. honey	1 small dish for beating egg
1 tbs. baking powder	1 fork
1 tsp. salt	1 large spoon for mixing
1 egg, well beaten	1 muffin tin with 12 cups
1 cup milk	1 cake rack
3 tbs. vegetable or nut oil	measuring cup
	measuring spoons

1. Preheat oven to 425° F.
2. Put the corn meal, flour, honey, baking powder, and salt into the large mixing bowl and mix well with a fork.
3. Into the medium mixing bowl, put the beaten egg, milk, and oil. Mix well.
4. Add the egg/milk/oil mixture to the corn meal/flour mixture and stir only until all ingredients are moistened.
5. Grease or oil the muffin tin (or line the cups with paper jackets).
6. Spoon the batter into the muffin cups until each one is ⅔ full.
7. Bake for 20 minutes at 425° or until the muffins are golden brown.
8. Cool on rack and serve slightly warm.

Blueberry Muffins

Homemade blueberry muffins served warm with honey and butter or margarine are a mouth-watering treat you should not miss.

12 muffins

INGREDIENTS

2 cups sifted unbleached flour

3 tsp. baking powder

3 tbs. honey

½ tsp. salt

¾ tsp. cinnamon

¾ cup milk

1 well-beaten egg

½ cup vegetable or nut oil

1 cup blueberries (cleaned and rinsed)

EQUIPMENT

1 large mixing bowl

1 medium mixing bowl

1 large spoon for mixing

sifter or sieve

1 muffin tin with 12 cups

1 fork for beating egg

measuring cup

measuring spoons

cake rack

1. Preheat oven to 400° F.
2. Combine the sifted flour, baking powder, salt, and cinnamon and sift into the large mixing bowl.
3. In the medium mixing bowl, mix together the beaten egg, milk, and honey.
4. Add the egg/milk/honey mixture to the flour mixture and stir well.
5. Add the oil to the batter and mix vigorously.
6. Fold the blueberries into the batter.
7. Grease or oil the muffin tins (or line each one with a paper jacket).
8. Spoon the batter into the muffin cups so that each cup is ¾ full.

9. Bake for 25 minutes or until puffy and light brown on top. Test with a toothpick.
10. Cool on rack and serve warm.

Scones

Scones are a treat from the British Isles. They are more of a muffin than a roll so they are included here. Scones are mostly eaten in Great Britain with afternoon tea but they are great for breakfast or any inbetween meal snack especially when they are spread with a favorite jam.

10–12 scones

INGREDIENTS	EQUIPMENT
2 cups unbleached flour	1 large mixing bowl
¼ cup honey plus some extra honey	1 small mixing bowl
1 tbs. baking powder	1 large spoon for mixing
1 tsp. salt	2 table knives
⅓ cup butter or margarine (room temperature)	pastry brush
¼ cup currants or raisins	spatula
2 eggs	baking sheet or large baking pan
⅓ cup milk (approximately)	1 large knife
	measuring cup
	measuring spoons
	wire whisk or egg beater
	1 fork
	cake rack

1. Preheat oven to 425° F.
2. In the large mixing bowl, combine the flour, honey, baking powder, and salt. Mix together with a fork.
3. Cut in the butter or margarine with 2 knives until the mixture looks like a bowlful of large crumbs.
4. Add the currants or raisins and stir a few times.
5. In the small mixing bowl, beat the two eggs with the whisk or egg beater until they are fluffy.
6. Add ⅓ cup of milk to the eggs and blend together well.
7. Pour the milk/egg mixture into the flour mixture and stir until the flour is moistened. You want to get a soft dough so if the mixture is still too crumbly, add a little more milk.

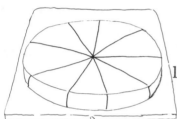

8. Lightly flour a clean surface and turn the soft dough onto it.
9. Knead the dough very gently for about 30 seconds.
10. Put the dough onto an *ungreased* cookie sheet (or into a large baking pan) and pat it out until it forms an 8-inch circle which is about ½ inch thick.
11. Dust flour on your large knife and cut 10 or 12 pie-shaped wedges into the circle.
12. Do not separate the wedges.
13. Brush the top of the scones with the extra honey.
14. Bake for 12 to 15 minutes in a 425° oven or until they are golden brown and a toothpick comes out clean.
15. Remove from the pan or the cookie sheet with a spatula and cool down on a cake rack. Serve warm or cold, or toasted.

Yoghurt Raisin Nut Muffins

This quick, easy recipe makes unusual muffins which are as good for you as they are good to eat.

12 muffins

INGREDIENTS	EQUIPMENT
1½ cups whole-wheat or un-bleached flour	1 muffin tin with 12 cups
¼ cup molasses	1 large mixing bowl
1 cup yoghurt	1 medium mixing bowl
2 eggs lightly beaten	sifter or sieve
2 tbs. vegetable or nut oil	1 large spoon for mixing
¼ cup raisins	1 fork for beating egg
¼ cup chopped nuts	1 small dish for beating egg
1 tsp. salt	measuring cup
2 tbs. soy powder (optional)	measuring spoons
1 tbs. baking powder	cake rack

1. Preheat oven to 375° F.
2. In the large bowl, mix together the eggs and the yoghurt.
3. Add the oil and molasses, and beat well with the large spoon.
4. Sift together the flour, soy powder, salt, and baking powder in the medium bowl.
5. Slowly add the flour mixture to the egg/yoghurt/molasses/oil mixture and mix well.
6. Stir in the raisins and the nuts and mix thoroughly.
7. Oil or grease the muffin tins (or line them with paper jackets).
8. Spoon the batter into each muffin cup until each cup is ⅔ full.
9. Bake for 20 minutes at 375° or until done.
10. Cool on rack and serve warm or cold.

Cupcakes and Muffins

14

Cakes and Cookies

CAKES

Before cake baking became a popular, separate art, people made sweet cake or "fancy bread," as they called it, by adding other ingredients to a portion of leftover bread dough.

As people became more interested in these fancy breads, they began to experiment. They found that they could use many eggs or brandy or sack (a type of alcoholic beverage) instead of yeast to make a fancy bread rise. Some of the earliest cakes that used ingredients other than yeast for rising are still baked today—such as fruit cakes and pound cakes. People also discovered that eggs beaten into a foam caused a cake to rise and invented the ancestors of our modern angel cake and sponge cake.

Today there are more kinds of cakes around than a person could taste in a lifetime. The word cake is used to describe a dessert or sweet made of flour, honey or sugar, shortening, eggs, seasoning and, usually, some leavening and liquid. A cake can have a single layer or many layers; icing, filling, or no adornments at all. It can be square, round, high (like a wedding cake), rolled (like a sponge layer cake), or very small (like a cupcake). Whatever its shape or size, a homemade cake is a special treat. If you buy a packaged cake mix, it will be loaded with sugar, preservative, and substitutes for real flavoring such as vanilla-type flavoring or artificial almond flavoring. The final product will always taste a bit like the cellophane wrapped packaged cakes that can be bought in supermarkets.

If you bake your own cake, you know that all ingredients in it are fresh, healthy for you, and real. The difference in taste between the cake you make yourself from scratch and one you whip up from a packaged mix can only be believed after you take your first bite.

COOKIES

The word "cookie" comes from a Dutch word *koekje* which means little cake. The ingredients in cookies are similar to those found in cakes however there are many more ways to bake cookies.

Some cookies are made on the top of the stove, some are dropped in tiny globs onto a cookie sheet, and some can be shaped into any imaginable thing from rolled dough. Cookies can be soft to bite into, crunchy and hard, crumbly, spicy, sweet, filled with fruit or nuts, plain, or iced. Whatever the shape, form, or texture, cookies made at home by you will be better in taste and in nutritional value than any packaged cookies you can buy in a store.

Old-Fashioned Gingerbread

If you make this gingerbread recipe, serve it with heaping spoonfuls of spicy applesauce topped with whipped cream. The combination is guaranteed to make your mouth water.

6–8 servings

INGREDIENTS	EQUIPMENT
2⅓ cups unbleached flour	small saucepan
½ cup molasses	1 9-inch square baking pan
¾ cup honey	1 large spoon for mixing
½ cup butter or margarine	1 large mixing bowl
1 tsp. baking soda	sifter or sieve
1½ tsp. ground ginger	cake rack
1 tsp. cinnamon	measuring spoons
¼ tsp. ground cloves	measuring cup
1 cup sour cream	
pinch of salt	

1. Preheat oven to 350° F.
2. Put the molasses and shortening into the saucepan and heat them until they boil. Turn off heat as soon as the mixture boils and remove the pot from the stove.
3. Sift the flour, spices, and pinch of salt into the large mixing bowl.
4. When the molasses/shortening mixture has cooled slightly, add the sour cream to it. Stir well.
5. Add the molasses/shortening/sour cream mixture to the flour mixture and stir until you have a smooth batter.
6. Add the honey to the mixture and blend together well.
7. Grease your baking pan very well.
8. Spoon the batter into the baking pan.

9. Bake at 350° for 35 to 40 minutes or until done.
10. Cool in the pan on the cake rack.
11. It is easier to serve gingerbread directly from the baking pan. Slice it into squares and heap each square with applesauce and whipped cream.

Raisin Loaf Cake

Raisin loaf cake is so often sold in small, cellophane packages that one can almost believe that is the only way it comes. Try making this raisin cake at home and see for yourself how good raisin cake can taste. This is a very slow cooking recipe so allow enough time for the required two-hour baking.

1 large loaf

INGREDIENTS	EQUIPMENT
3 cups sifted unbleached flour	1 large knife for chopping raisins
½ cup butter or margarine	1 small mixing bowl for beating eggs
½ cup vegetable or nut oil	1 fork or wire whisk
1 cup honey	1 heavy spoon for creaming
4 eggs, well beaten	1 large spoon for mixing
3 tsp. baking powder	1 large mixing bowl
½ tsp. salt	sifter or sieve
1 tsp. vanilla extract	2 medium bowls for sifting flour
1 tsp. lemon extract	1 large loaf pan
1 cup raisins, chopped	measuring cup
	measuring spoons
	cake rack

1. Preheat oven to 300° F.
2. In the large mixing bowl, cream the butter or margarine with the honey until it is smooth and fluffy.
3. Add the oil to the mixture and blend in well.
4. Add the beaten eggs to the shortening/honey mixture and stir very well.
5. Sift the already sifted and measured flour *two more times* with the baking powder and salt.
6. Slowly add the flour mixture to the shortening/honey/ egg mixture, stirring constantly.
7. Beat the batter until it is smooth.
8. Add the vanilla and lemon extracts and stir in well.
9. Fold in the raisins.
10. Grease the loaf pan.
11. Pour the batter into the loaf pan and bake for 2 hours at 300° F. or until done.
12. Cool for a few minutes in the pan on a rack, remove the cake from the pan, and cool it completely on the rack.
13. No icing is necessary for this cake.

Fruit Cake

This fruit cake can be served plain or with an icing on it. If you decide to ice it, try a cream cheese icing and store the cake in the refrigerator.

1 medium loaf

INGREDIENTS	EQUIPMENT
2 cups sifted whole-wheat or un-bleached flour	1 medium bowl for sifting flour
½ cup butter or margarine	1 large mixing bowl
1 cup honey	sifter or sieve
	1 heavy spoon for creaming

INGREDIENTS	EQUIPMENT
1 egg	1 large spoon for mixing
½ cup buttermilk (or sour cream)	1 medium loaf pan
1 cup chopped dried fruit (any kind)	1 egg beater (optional)
½ tsp. cinnamon	measuring cup
½ tsp. nutmeg	measuring spoons
¼ tsp. salt	1 large knife for chopping fruit
1 tsp. baking soda	cake rack

1. Preheat oven to 325° F.
2. In the large bowl, cream together the shortening and honey until they are smooth.
3. Beat in the egg and keep beating until fluffy.
4. Add the sifted flour, buttermilk, baking soda, salt, nutmeg, and cinnamon. Mix very well until smooth.
5. Fold in the fruit.
6. Grease or oil the loaf pan.
7. Spoon the batter into the loaf pan.
8. Bake for about 1¼ hours or until a toothpick comes out clean.
9. Cool on a cake rack and ice if you want to.

Orange Cake

This is a cake which is soaked in a wonderful syrup and served with whipped cream or ice cream. It's baked in a ring pan which is a pan with a cylinder in the middle of it. It makes the cake have a hole in its center. If you do not have such a pan, you can bake this cake in two 8-inch round cake pans.

6–8 servings

INGREDIENTS

Syrup:

¾ cup honey

1 tbs. frozen concentrated orange
  juice, thawed

¼ cup water

Cake:

¾ cup butter or margarine

¾ cup honey

3 eggs

1 cup unbleached flour

1 cup chopped walnuts or pecans

1 tsp. grated orange rind

1½ tsp. baking powder

¼ tsp. salt

½ tsp. cinnamon

½ tsp. nutmeg

2 tbs. milk

2 tbs. frozen concentrated orange
  juice, thawed

EQUIPMENT

1 8-inch ring pan or 2 8-inch round
  cake pans

1 small saucepan

1 large mixing bowl

1 medium-sized mixing bowl

sifter or sieve

1 large spoon for mixing

1 heavy spoon for creaming

egg beater or electric mixer

large platter

measuring cup

measuring spoons

1. Syrup: In the small saucepan, simmer the honey and ¼
   cup of water for 3 minutes. Add the tablespoon of concentrated orange juice. Stir and simmer for another
   minute. Set aside and let cool.
2. Preheat oven to 350° F.
3. In the large mixing bowl, cream the butter or margarine and the honey until it is smooth.
4. Using the egg beater or an electric mixer, beat in the
   eggs one at a time. Set aside.

5. Sift the flour, baking powder, salt, and spices into the medium mixing bowl.

6. Add some of the flour mixture to the shortening/honey/egg mixture and mix well with the large spoon.

7. Add some of the milk to this batter and stir well.

8. Add some of the orange juice concentrate to the batter and mix well.

9. Keep repeating steps 6, 7, and 8 until all of the flour, milk, and orange concentrate are in the batter.

10. Fold in the orange rind and the chopped nuts.

11. Grease and dust with flour the 8-inch ring pan or the two 8-inch cake pans.

12. Pour the batter into your pan or pans.

13. Bake at 350° for 30 minutes or until done.

14. Remove the cake from the oven and let it stand for a few minutes to cool.

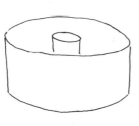

15. Remove it from the pan or pans while it is still fairly hot and place the cake on a large dish (two dishes if you have two layers).

16. Pour the syrup over the hot cake and let it soak in.

17. Before serving, fill the center of the ring cake with whipped cream or slightly softened ice cream. If you have two plain layers, put the whipped cream on the top of one layer and then place the second layer on top of the cream, making a layer cake.

18. If there is leftover cake, keep it in the refrigerator.

Peanut Butter Cake

This cake is baked in a loaf pan but it is definitely a cake and not a bread. Ice it with a favorite icing or, if you wish, cut it in half and make a layer cake out of it. Try the raisin coconut icing or a raisin or dried fruit filling and the honey frosting.

1 medium loaf

INGREDIENTS

2 cups whole-wheat or unbleached
   flour
4 tsp. baking powder
½ tsp. salt
¾ cup honey
⅔ cup peanut butter
1¼ cups plain yoghurt
2 tbs. vegetable or nut oil

EQUIPMENT

sifter or sieve
1 large spoon for mixing
1 large mixing bowl
1 medium loaf pan
cake rack
1 medium mixing bowl
measuring cup
measuring spoons

1. Preheat oven to 350° F.
2. Sift together the flour, baking powder, and salt into the medium mixing bowl.
3. Mix together the honey, peanut butter, oil, and yoghurt in the large mixing bowl until they are thoroughly blended.
4. Slowly add the flour mixture to the honey/peanut butter/yoghurt mixture, stirring constantly until the batter is well blended.
5. Oil or grease the loaf pan.
6. Spoon the batter into the pan.
7. Bake for 50 minutes at 350° or until done.
8. Cool on a cake rack and then ice.
9. Store this cake in a moisture-proof wrapper or in a special cake storage dish. If you ice it, store it in the refrigerator.

Carrot Layer Cake

Carrots are naturally sweet and have a flavor which easily lends itself to foods such as cakes. This cake is particularly delicious when filled and iced with thick honey frosting.

INGREDIENTS

1⅓ cups unbleached flour

1 cup honey

3 eggs

1 cup vegetable or nut oil

¼ cup dry milk powder

2 tsp. baking powder

1 tsp. baking soda

1⅓ tsp. cinnamon

½ tsp. salt

2 cups grated carrots (or 1½ cups
  mashed, cooked carrots)

½ cup chopped nuts

¾ cup chopped currants or raisins

EQUIPMENT

1 large knife for chopping

egg beater or electric mixer

sifter or sieve

grater (if you are using raw carrots)

1 large mixing bowl

1 large spoon for mixing

2 9-inch round layer cake pans

1 medium mixing bowl

cake rack

measuring cup

measuring spoons

1. Preheat oven to 300° F.
2. In the medium mixing bowl, sift together the flour, dry milk powder, baking soda, baking powder, cinnamon, and salt.
3. In the large bowl, combine the honey and the oil. Mix well.
4. Beat the eggs into the honey/oil mixture one at a time, using the egg beater or electric mixer.
5. Add the flour mixture to the oil/honey/egg mixture and beat very well.
6. Fold in the carrots, nuts, and currants or raisins.
7. Oil or grease the baking pans.
8. Pour the batter into the baking pans (half of the batter in each pan).
9. Bake for one hour or until done in a 300° F. oven.
10. Cool on a cake rack and ice.

Cakes and Cookies

Sponge Roll Cake

This almost flourless recipe makes a light, pliable cake which is rolled into small, individual servings with your choice of filling. It takes a little care in the rolling process but the time you spend doing it is made up in the 10 minute baking time.

16 servings

INGREDIENTS
¼ cup unbleached flour
¼ cup honey
¼ cup cornstarch
4 eggs, separated
½ tsp. vanilla
½ tsp. grated lemon rind
¼ tsp. lemon juice

EQUIPMENT
sifter or sieve
2 dishes for separated eggs
egg beater or electric mixer
1 large spoon for mixing
1 clean sheet of brown paper, 11x16 inches (part of a paper bag) or waxed paper
fork
2 medium mixing bowls
11x16-inch baking pan
cake rack
measuring cup
measuring spoons
sharp knife
spatula

1. Preheat oven to 400° F.
2. In a medium mixing bowl, sift the cornstarch and flour together and set aside.
3. In the other medium mixing bowl, beat the egg whites with the egg beater (or electric mixer) until they form soft peaks.

4. Gradually add the honey to the egg whites and keep beating until the mixture is stiff.
5. With a fork, beat the egg yolks slightly.
6. Take 1 cup of the egg white/honey mixture and gently stir it into the egg yolks.
7. Then take the egg white/egg yolk mixture and pour it back into the egg white/honey mixture. Stir a few times.
8. Add the flour and cornstarch to the egg/honey mixture and stir.
9. Fold in the lemon juice, lemon rind, and vanilla.
10. Grease your baking pan and line the bottom of it with a sheet of clean, smooth brown paper.

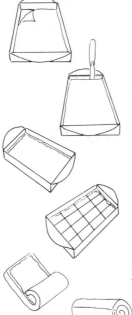

11. Grease the paper.
12. Spoon the batter into the pan and gently spread it evenly over the bottom of the pan.
13. Bake for 10 minutes at 400° or until it is done.
14. Cool the sponge cake in its pan on a cake rack.
15. When it is cool, gently ease a knife around the sides of the pan to make sure that the cake is not sticking to the pan.
16. Spread your favorite filling or icing over the entire surface of the cake.*
17. With a clean knife, make three cuts going lengthwise and three running the width of the cake so that you divide the cake into 16 pieces (see illustration).
18. Lift the pieces out one at a time (with the help of a dull knife) and roll each piece tightly. The icing will "glue" the pieces of cake so that they won't unroll.

* Try the cream cheese frosting (use ½ the recipe) or the fruit fillings or the dried fruit whip or even homemade applesauce to fill this cake.

Cakes and Cookies

Pumpkin Layer Cake

Pumpkin is a very versatile food and it adds a wonderful flavor to a cake. However, if you are using canned pumpkin, be sure that you buy pure pumpkin and not pumpkin pie filling. If you want to cook your own pumpkin, see the recipe for cooking pumpkin in the pie section.

INGREDIENTS	EQUIPMENT
2 cups sifted unbleached flour	sifter or sieve
2/3 cup cooked, mashed pumpkin (or canned pumpkin)	1 dish for beating eggs
	1 fork for beating eggs
1/2 cup milk	1 large mixing bowl
1 cup honey	1 medium mixing bowl
1/2 cup butter or margarine	1 heavy spoon for creaming
3 tsp. baking powder	1 large spoon for mixing
1/4 tsp. salt	2 8-inch round layer cake pans
1/4 tsp. ground cloves	cake rack
1 1/2 tsp. cinnamon	measuring cup
1/2 tsp. nutmeg	measuring spoons
1/2 tsp. ginger	
2 eggs, well beaten	

1. Preheat oven to 350° F.
2. Into the medium mixing bowl, sift together the sifted flour, baking powder, salt, cinnamon, cloves, nutmeg, and ginger.
3. In the large bowl, cream together the butter or margarine and honey.
4. When the shortening/honey mixture is well blended, add the beaten eggs and pumpkin. Blend together very well.

5. Add some of the flour mixture to the shortening/honey/egg/pumpkin mixture and stir well.
6. Add some of the milk to the mixture. Stir well.
7. Keep adding the flour mixture and the milk until all ingredients are in one bowl. Stir very thoroughly.
8. Grease your baking pans and dust them with flour.
9. Pour the batter into the pans (half of the batter in each pan).
10. Bake for 30 to 35 minutes or until done at 350° F.
11. Cool on a cake rack and ice with your favorite frosting. Or, if you wish, you can put a filling between the layers and ice only the outside of the cake. Try the dried fruit filling and the cream cheese frosting.

Quick Carob Cake

Here is a cake for you to make if you are in a hurry. It takes no time to mix and only about 30 minutes to bake. While it is baking, you can whip up a delicious icing for it.

INGREDIENTS	EQUIPMENT
1½ cups sifted unbleached flour	1 medium mixing bowl
2 tbs. carob powder	1 large spoon for mixing
1 tsp. baking soda	sifter or sieve
¾ cup honey	1 9x9-inch square baking pan
½ tsp. salt	cake rack
5 tbs. vegetable or nut oil	measuring spoons
1 tsp. vanilla	measuring cup
1 cup milk	

1. Preheat oven to 350° F.
2. Put the sifted flour back into the sifter or sieve with the baking soda, salt, and carob powder and sift.
3. Add the oil, honey, vanilla, and milk to the flour mixture and mix with the large spoon until the batter is smooth.
4. Grease the baking pan.
5. Pour your batter into the baking pan.
6. Bake for 30 minutes or until done at 350° F.
7. Cool on the cake rack for about 10 minutes and then remove the cake from the pan. Finish cooling on the rack.
8. Try the no-cook carob frosting (use ½ the recipe since this is a single layer), and garnish the top of the cake with chopped nuts.

Chestnut Cakes

These small, delicate-tasting cakes originated in India. No flour is needed to make them but you do need some muscle power. Use only fresh chestnuts which can be found in their shells in many supermarkets around Thanksgiving and Christmas. Most people use the chestnuts for stuffing holiday birds or simply for eating after they have been roasted. However, this sweet, soft nut has a number of other uses—such as the main ingredient in these cakes.

INGREDIENTS	EQUIPMENT
25 chestnuts	1 mortar and pestle (or one hammer that as been cleaned very well and a wooden bowl or board)
½ cup honey	
1 tbs. vegetable or nut oil	
3 tbs. heavy cream	
1 egg, separated	1 medium mixing bowl
1 tsp. almond extract	1 cookie sheet or large baking pan
1 tsp. orange extract	2 small dishes for separated egg

EQUIPMENT

spatula

1 large spoon for mixing

measuring cup

measuring spoons

paring knife

fork

pastry brush

cake rack

---

1. Preheat oven to 275° F.
2. Make a long slit in each chestnut with a knife. This prevents them from exploding.
3. Place the chestnuts on the cookie sheet and bake them for 15 minutes.
4. Remove them from the oven and let them cool for about 10 minutes. Leave the oven on.
5. Peel the chestnuts.
6. Pound the chestnuts (a few at a time) with your mortar and pestle or with the hammer on a board or in a wooden bowl until they are soft.
7. Put the pounded chestnuts into a mixing bowl and add the egg white. Mix very well.
8. When the egg white/chestnut mixture is very smooth, add the honey, cream, extracts, and oil. Mix together very well.
9. Oil or grease the cookie sheet.
10. Roll the chestnut batter into small balls and place them on the cookie sheet.
11. Flatten each ball slightly with your fingers.
12. Beat the egg yolk with a fork and brush it on each cake.
13. Bake for 10 minutes or until light brown on top at 275°, and remove with a spatula.
14. Cool on a cake rack.

Almond Cookies

This recipe is one of the many recipes which exist for Chinese Almond Cookies. These are thick, chewy cookies that make a fine dessert or filling snack.

About 20 cookies

INGREDIENTS	EQUIPMENT
1½ cups unbleached flour	1 large mixing bowl
⅓ cup butter or margarine	1 medium mixing bowl
½ cup honey	1 small bowl for beating egg
1 egg	1 fork for beating egg
⅓ tsp. baking powder	sifter or sieve
¼ tsp. vanilla extract	rolling pin
¾ tsp. almond extract	round cookie cutter or drinking glass
pinch of salt	spatula
20 whole almonds (shelled)	egg beater
	2 cookie sheets (or 1 cookie sheet and you can make several batches)
	1 large spoon for mixing
	measuring cup
	measuring spoons
	cake rack

1. Preheat oven to 350° F.
2. Into the medium mixing bowl, sift the flour, baking powder, and salt.
3. In the large mixing bowl, cream the butter or margarine and honey. When it is smooth, beat it with the egg beater until the mixture is very smooth.

4. In the small bowl, beat the egg with a fork or beater until it is fluffy.
5. Add the egg, vanilla, and almond extracts to the shortening/honey mixture. Stir well.
6. Slowly add the flour mixture to the egg/shortening/honey mixture, stirring constantly.
7. When all the ingredients are mixed thoroughly, begin gently kneading the dough with your hands. Add some extra flour if the dough is too sticky.
8. Keep gently kneading the dough until it is firm.
9. Sprinkle flour on a clean surface and turn the dough onto it.
10. Rub flour on your rolling pin and roll out the dough until it is ½ inch thick.
11. Using a round cookie cutter or the top of a drinking glass, cut the rolled dough into round shapes.
12. Don't throw away any dough. Pick up the left over dough, make a ball out of it, roll it again, and cut some more cookies.
13. Grease your cookie sheets (or a large baking pan).
14. Place the cookies on the cookie sheet and put an almond in the center of each cookie. Press it down gently into the cookie.
15. Bake for 25 minutes at 350° or until light brown.
16. If you have to make your cookies in several batches, cover the unbaked cookies with some cellophane wrap or tin foil so that they won't dry out.
17. Cool these cookies on a cake rack.

Fortune Cookies

You can have some fun with your family and friends with these cookies. Before you begin baking them, write out fortunes on 18 small pieces of paper (about ½x1½ inches).

Set these aside within easy reach because you will be inserting them in the cookies as you make them.

18 cookies

INGREDIENTS	EQUIPMENT
2 eggs	egg beater or electric mixer
⅓ cup honey	1 medium bowl
⅓ cup unbleached flour	1 large, heavy frying pan or 1 electric pancake grill
⅓ tsp. banana or lemon extract	spatula
	measuring spoons
	measuring cup
	cake rack

1. Beat the eggs with the egg beater or the electric mixer for two minutes.
2. Add the honey gradually to the eggs and beat for 10 *minutes* more.
3. Slowly add the flour to the egg/honey mixture after the 10 minutes of beating. Keep beating until the mixture is smooth.
4. Add the extract and beat for 2 more minutes.
5. Warm the frying pan over a *low heat* (or turn the electric grill on to low).

6. Drop the cookie batter by tablespoons into the frying pan or onto the electric grill. Make sure that you leave space between cookies; you don't want them running into each other in the pan. You will have to make several batches.

7. Toast the cookies about ½ minute on each side. Turn them over with the spatula. Keep cooking and turning them until they are light brown. This should only take a few minutes.

8. As each panful is toasted and while the cookies are still hot, remove the cookies, place them on a clean surface and place a strip of your fortune telling paper into the center of each. Fold up the cookies.
9. Put the cookies on a rack to cool.
10. Make another batch.

Almond Macaroons

Macaroons are a very old kind of cookie. They are mostly honey and nuts; the egg whites in them cause them to rise a bit. If you've never had them, try making these unique cookies. If you've tasted store-bought macaroons, you'll be surprised by the fresh good taste of your homemade cookies. These macaroons resemble traditional cookies more than store-bought puffy little macaroon cakes. Keep them in an air-tight container so that they remain soft.

About 3 dozen cookies

INGREDIENTS

1 cup (4 oz. package) of ground almonds

½ cup honey

¾ cup flour

¼ tsp. baking soda

½ cup shredded unsweetened coconut

¼ tsp. salt

2 egg whites

¼ tsp. almond extract

30 blanched almond halves

EQUIPMENT

2 cookie sheets or 2 large baking pans

1 egg beater or electric mixer

1 small mixing bowl

1 large mixing bowl

1 large spoon for mixing

measuring spoons

measuring cup

cake rack

spatula

1. Preheat oven to 300° F.
2. In the small mixing bowl, beat the egg whites with the egg beater or electric mixer until the whites stand in soft peaks. Set aside.
3. In the large bowl, mix together the ground almonds, coconut, honey, flour, extract, and salt.
4. Add the beaten egg whites to the almond/coconut/flour mixture. Stir with the large spoon.
5. Lightly grease your cookie sheets or baking pans.
6. Drop the batter by *teaspoonsful* onto your cookie sheets or baking pans. It is very important for you to have at least 2 inches between each macaroon.
7. Gently press an almond half into the top of each macaroon.
8. Bake near the *bottom* of your oven for 25 minutes or until the macaroons are *very delicately* browned.
9. Remove from oven and use a spatula to place the macaroons on the cake rack to cool.
10. Remember to store them in a tightly sealed container after they have cooled.

Manus's Favorite Carob Cookies

Everyone has a favorite cookie. These crisp and chewy carob cookies are what my husband Manus means when he says, "Why don't you make me some cookies?"

About 8 dozen cookies

INGREDIENTS	EQUIPMENT
1⅛ cups unbleached or whole-wheat pastry flour	1 large mixing bowl
3 tbs. carob powder	1 medium mixing bowl
¾ cup honey	1 large spoon for mixing
½ cup margarine or butter	1 heavy spoon for creaming
¼ tsp. baking soda	2 cookie sheets or two large baking pans

INGREDIENTS	EQUIPMENT
½ tsp. baking powder	measuring cup
1½ tsp. vanilla	measuring spoons
1 egg	cake rack
	sifter or sieve
	spatula

1. Preheat oven to 400° F.
2. Sift together flour, carob powder, baking powder, and baking soda in medium mixing bowl.
3. In large mixing bowl, cream together shortening and honey until mixture is smooth.
4. Add the egg to the shortening/honey mixture and blend together thoroughly.
5. Add dry ingredients to the egg/shortening/honey mixture and stir very well.
6. Stir in the vanilla and mix thoroughly.
7. Grease the cookie sheets or large baking pans.
8. Drop the batter by ½ teaspoonful onto the baking sheets leaving at least 1½ inches between cookies.
9. Bake 8 to 10 minutes in a 400° oven or until cookies are a slightly darker brown around the edges than they are in the middle.
10. Remove from cookie sheets with a spatula and cool on a rack.
11. You will probably have to make several batches of these small, lacy cookies.

Coconut Cookies

These simple, flaky cookies take a bit more time to prepare than some of the other cookies in this book. Make allowances for the hour and a half the cookie dough must spend in a freezer.

INGREDIENTS

2¼ cups unbleached flour

1 stick (¼ lb.) margarine or butter

½ cup vegetable or nut oil

3 tbs. honey

1 cup flaked, unsweetened coconut

EQUIPMENT

1 heavy spoon for creaming

1 large mixing bowl

waxed paper or tinfoil

1 large, sharp knife

2 cookie sheets or 2 large baking pans

spatula

cake rack

1. Cream together the margarine or butter and the oil until smooth.
2. Add the honey and mix well.
3. Add the flour and coconut and cream the entire mixture until it is smooth.
4. Divide the dough in half and make two fat sausagelike rolls.
5. Wrap each roll in waxed paper or tin foil.
6. Place the dough rolls in the freezer for 1½ hours.
7. After 1½ hours, remove the dough from the freezer and unwrap it.
8. Preheat oven to 375° F.
9. With the large, sharp knife, slice cookies (about ¼ inch thick) from the rolls.
10. Place the cookies on ungreased cookie sheets or in large baking pans and bake for 20 minutes at 375° or until they are *very light* brown.
11. Remove from sheet or pan with spatula.
12. Cool on a cake rack.
13. You may have to make more than one batch of these if you only have one cookie sheet or large baking pan.

No-Flour Nut Cookies

These unusual nut cookies are almost like a baked candy. If you're tired of the heavier flour cookies, try these for a change.

INGREDIENTS	EQUIPMENT
3 egg whites	1 egg beater or electric mixer
4 tbs. honey	1 large bowl
2 tbs. grated lemon rind	1 large spoon for mixing
2 cups ground almonds or walnuts	1 or 2 cookie sheets or large baking pans
	spatula
	cake rack
	measuring cup
	measuring spoons

1. Preheat oven to 350° F.
2. In the large bowl, beat the egg whites until they are stiff but not dry.
3. Add the honey slowly to the stiff egg whites and beat steadily.
4. Gently fold in the lemon rind and the nuts.
5. Grease the cookie sheets or baking pans.
6. Drop batter by teaspoonsful onto the cookie sheet or into the baking pans. Leave about 1 inch between the cookies.
7. Bake for 10 minutes in a 350° oven or until delicately brown.
8. Remove with a spatula and cool on a cake rack.
9. Make several batches if you run out of space on your available cookie sheet or baking pan.

Spice Cookies

You can really exercise your artistic abilities with these thin spice cookies. Cut them into fancy shapes, make them large or small, and store them in an airtight container when they have cooled. This recipe makes about 36 small crunchy cookies which will keep for a number of weeks in their container. It is doubtful, however, that there will be any left for that long.

INGREDIENTS	EQUIPMENT
2½ cups sifted whole-wheat pastry flour (or unbleached flour)	1 small saucepan
⅝ cup molasses	1 large mixing bowl
⅜ cup honey	waxed paper or tin foil
½ cup butter or margarine	rolling pin
½ tsp. salt	1 small sharp knife
½ tsp. baking soda	cookie sheet or large baking pan
1 tsp. ginger	spatula
½ tsp. cinnamon	cake rack
½ tsp. ground cloves	1 large spoon for mixing
	sifter or sieve

1. In the saucepan, melt the butter or margarine over a low heat.
2. Add the honey and molasses to the melted shortening and stir. Set aside.
3. Sift the flour, salt, baking soda, and spices together into the large mixing bowl.
4. Add the molasses/honey/shortening mixture to the flour mixture and mix thoroughly until you have a smooth dough.
5. If your dough seems runny, add a bit more flour until you have a firm dough that is not sticky.

6. Wrap the dough in waxed paper or tin foil and chill for 1 hour in the refrigerator. (You can leave this dough in the refrigerator for several days if you wish.)
7. Preheat oven to 375° F.
8. Flour a clean surface. Unwrap the dough and divide it into 4 equal parts. Leave 3 parts in the refrigerator and work with one portion of dough at a time.
9. Place the portion of dough on the floured surface and pat it down. Cover it with a large sheet of waxed paper. If you don't have waxed paper, flour your rolling pin.
10. Roll out the dough to ⅛ inch thickness. Peel off the waxed paper.
11. Cut the dough into fancy shapes.
12. Grease a cookie sheet or a large baking pan.
13. Place your cookies on the baking sheet and bake for 10 minutes at 375°. (You may need the help of your spatula to lift these cookies off the table and into the pan.)
14. While the first batch is baking, begin rolling and cutting the second batch of cookies. Don't forget to watch the clock. These are very thin cookies and can overcook or burn easily. You can tell when these cookies are done because they will be a golden brown in the center and a slightly darker brown around the edges.
15. Remember to grease the cookie sheet or baking pan between batches.
16. Remove the cookies with a spatula and let them cool on a rack.

Fruit Pinwheel Cookies

Filled cookies are not difficult to make—they just take a bit more time than the ordinary cookie. If you have an afternoon to spend in the kitchen or a special occasion to cook for, try these very pretty, very good cookies.

INGREDIENTS

Filling:

1 8-oz. package of dried apricots, peaches, or raisins, finely chopped

¼ cup honey

½ cup chopped pecans or walnuts

⅛ cup water

Dough:

2¾ cups unbleached flour

½ tsp. baking soda

½ tsp. salt

½ cup butter or margarine (room temperature)

¾ cup honey

½ tsp. vanilla extract

EQUIPMENT

2 medium mixing bowls

1 small mixing bowl

1 large knife for chopping fruit

sifter or sieve

1 large spoon for mixing

egg beater or electric mixer

rolling pin

waxed paper

cookie sheets or large baking pans

spatula

measuring cup

measuring spoons

cake rack

Filling:

1. Combine the fruit (finely chopped) and the honey in the small bowl.
2. Stir in the nuts, and set aside.

Dough:

3. Sift the flour, salt, and baking soda into one bowl. Set aside.
4. In a separate bowl, cream the butter or margarine and the honey until smooth.

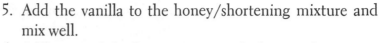

5. Add the vanilla to the honey/shortening mixture and mix well.
6. Add some of the flour mixture to the honey/shortening mixture and mix very well.
7. Keep adding the flour mixture slowly until all ingredients are combined. Add a little extra flour if the dough is not firm.
8. Divide the dough into 4 parts.
9. Cut 2 sheets of waxed paper at least 7 inches wide and 10 inches long.
10. Place 1 portion of dough between the 2 sheets of waxed paper and roll with rolling pin until it forms an 8 x 6-inch rectangle.
11. Peel the top layer of waxed paper off and trim with a knife if necessary.
12. Spread ¼ of the filling over the entire surface of the rectangle.
13. Carefully roll up the rectangle tightly (roll along the wide end).
14. Wrap the roll in waxed paper and put in the freezer for 1 hour.
15. Repeat entire rolling and filling operation (steps 10 through 14) until all 4 portions of dough and all of the filling is used up.
16. After 1 hour, preheat oven to 375° F.
17. Remove dough from freezer, unwrap and slice the rolls into cookies that are ¼ inch thick.
18. Grease your cookie sheets or large baking pans.
19. Place the cookies on the sheets leaving 1 inch between cookies.
20. Bake them for 10 minutes or until they are golden brown.

21. Remove them from the sheets with a spatula and cool on a rack.
22. Since this recipe makes about 8 dozen cookies, you will be making several batches.
23. If you feel that this is too large a recipe simply cut it in half. Don't try to freeze the filled, uncooked rolls for more than two hours. The nuts in the filling will get soggy if you do.

15

Icings, Frostings, and Fillings

It would be silly to take the trouble to make a delicious cake that is also a healthy food and then cover it with sugar. However, most icing on cakes and cupcakes are made with a great deal of powdered or granulated sugar. This includes both soft and hard icings and all of the icing mixes sold in markets.

The icings in this chapter have no sugar in them. In fact, some of them may seem quite unusual to you because the ingredients in them are probably not what you are accustomed to eating on cakes. However, they will be as sweet, gooey, and delicious as any standard icing and perhaps even better.

While you are selecting an icing for your cake, glance through the chapter on whips and the chapter about fruit concoctions. Many cakes are great with cooked fruit filling and many whips make great filling and icing. For example, apricot whip and dried fruit cream whip make fine fillings and icings. The dried apricot, peach, or apple preserves, the naturally sweet fruit jam, or the fruit compote make fine cake fillings. Use your imagination and have fun.

Whipped Cream

Whipped cream made from scratch is about one thousand times better than any of the canned, pressurized products on the market. It is extremely simple to make and has no chemicals or sugar in it. You can flavor your whipped cream with extracts or even with a tablespoon of softened peanut butter. Plain or flavored, whipped cream is an old-fashioned delight.

INGREDIENTS	EQUIPMENT
½ pt. of heavy cream	1 medium mixing bowl
1 tsp. honey	1 egg beater or electric mixer
	measuring spoons

1. Pour the honey and the heavy cream into the bowl.
2. Beat with the egg beater or electric mixer until it is fluffy and holds its shape.
3. If you are using an electric beater that has its own bowl and stand, do not leave the cream whipping while you go do something else. If the cream whips for too long, it will become butter.
4. If you wish, add 1 tsp. of either lemon, orange, almond, or chocolate extract to the cream while you are whipping it. You can also add 1 tbs. of peanut butter during the whipping process for an unusual icing.

No-Cook Carob Frosting

Here is a creamy frosting for you if you crave a chocolate taste but do not want to chance the oily nature of chocolate.

INGREDIENTS	EQUIPMENT
⅔ cup dry, nonfat milk (powder)	1 heavy spoon for creaming
⅓ cup carob powder	egg beater or electric mixer
¼ cup honey	1 medium mixing bowl
¼ cup heavy cream	1 spoon and 1 table knife for
2 tbs. butter or margarine (room	spreading on frosting
temperature)	measuring cup
1 tsp. vanilla	measuring spoons
¼ cup chopped walnuts or pecans	
(optional)	

1. Cream together the shortening and the milk powder until smooth.
2. Stir in the carob powder until it is well blended.
3. Add the vanilla and the honey and beat until fluffy.
4. Slowly add the heavy cream and beat until the frosting is thick.
5. Carob frosting is enhanced further by a sprinkling of chopped walnuts or pecans over the finished cake. You can also mix ¼ cup of chopped nuts into the finished frosting.

This should cover a 2-layer 9-inch round cake.

Cream Cheese Frosting

If you frost a cake with cream cheese frosting, refrigerate it to keep it fresh. This frosting is especially good on the peanut butter or fruit cake, or any cake filled with a fruit filling. This is enough frosting to frost a round, two-layer cake.

INGREDIENTS

2 8-oz. packages of cream cheese
2 tbs. honey
¼ cup heavy cream

EQUIPMENT

1 medium mixing bowl
1 heavy spoon for creaming
egg beater or electric mixer
1 spoon and 1 table knife for spreading frosting
measuring cup
measuring spoons

1. Let the cream cheese stand outside the refrigerator until it is almost room temperature.
2. Put the cream cheese and honey in the bowl and cream it until it is well blended.
3. Add the heavy cream to the mixture and beat with an egg beater or electric mixer until the frosting is fluffy and holds its own shape. Add some extra cream if the mixture is too thick.
4. For a different flavor, you can add 1 tsp. of either lemon, orange, or almond extract during step 2. You may also try adding ¼ cup of chopped nuts which you can stir in after the frosting is whipped. If you like raisins or dried fruit, stir in ¼ cup of raisins or chopped dried fruit after the frosting is whipped. After the cake or cupcakes are frosted, you can garnish with fresh or dried fruits and nuts.

Honey Frosting

This light, sweet, fluffy frosting is enough for a two-layer cake including the center, the sides, and the top. Wait until your cake is cold to touch before spreading the frosting on it.

INGREDIENTS

2 egg whites

¼ tsp. salt

1 cup warm honey

½ tsp. almond extract

EQUIPMENT

1 small saucepan

1 medium-sized mixing bowl

egg beater or electric mixer

measuring cup

measuring spoons

1 table knife and one spoon for spreading on frosting

1. In the saucepan, warm the honey over a very low heat for about 1 minute. Remove from stove and set aside.
2. Put the egg whites into the mixing bowl with the salt and beat with the egg beater or electric mixer until stiff but not dry.
3. *Gradually* add the honey and the extract to the egg whites, beating constantly.
4. Keep beating until the frosting holds its shape (about 2½ minutes with an electric beater and about 4 minutes with an egg beater).

Other Flavors:
You can substitute ½ tsp. of lemon extract or vanilla extract for the almond extract.

Raisin Coconut Icing

You need a blender to make this icing. This recipe makes one cup of icing which is enough for a loaf cake or for the outside of a 2-layer cake. It is an excellent filling for the rolled sponge cake.

INGREDIENTS

1 cup raisins

1 cup shredded, unsweetened coconut

1 pt. plain yoghurt

EQUIPMENT

blender

1 medium mixing bowl

1 spoon for mixing

1 table knife and spoon for spreading icing

measuring cup

1. Put the raisins and coconut in the blender, cover, and blend on a high speed until you have a smooth mixture.
2. Spoon the raisin/coconut mixture into the mixing bowl and add the yoghurt a little at a time.
3. Mix with a spoon until the icing is smooth.

Banana Icing

This recipe can be used to frost an entire cake or it can be used as a filling for a cake. It is suggested that you store any cake frosted or filled with banana frosting in the refrigerator.

INGREDIENTS

2 ripe bananas

4 tbs. honey

a little milk

EQUIPMENT

1 medium mixing bowl

egg beater or electric mixer

1 fork

1 spoon and 1 knife for spreading frosting

measuring spoons

1. In the mixing bowl, mash the bananas with a fork until they are smooth.

2. Add the honey and stir with the fork.
3. With your beater, begin beating the bananas and honey while you gradually add a little milk.
4. Keep beating and keep adding tiny amounts of milk until the mixture is fluffy and a good spreading consistency.

Raisin Filling

It's sometimes nice to fill a layer cake with one type of ingredient and ice it with another. Here is a simple, sweet, juicy filling for you to try. This recipe makes approximately 2½ cupsful of filling. This is enough for two 9-inch round cakes or for the filling and topping on one 9-inch round layer cake.

INGREDIENTS	EQUIPMENT
2 cups raisins, ground in a grinder or blender or chopped finely	1 medium saucepan
½ cup honey	1 large spoon for stirring
2 tbs. unsweetened prune juice	1 grinder, blender, or large knife for chopping
1 tbs. lemon juice	measuring cup
1 tbs. orange juice	measuring spoons

1. Put the ground or chopped raisins in the saucepan with the honey, prune juice, lemon juice, and orange juice.
2. Bring the mixture to a boil and immediately turn down the heat to low.
3. Simmer for 15 minutes, *stirring constantly*.
4. Remove from the stove and cool.

Dried Fruit Filling

Here is a variation on the raisin filling. Use any dried fruit which suits you. Combine several kinds if you wish. This recipe makes about 2½ cupsful of filling—enough for 1 layer cake if used as a topping and filling or for 2 9-inch layer cakes if used as a filling.

INGREDIENTS	EQUIPMENT
2 cups ground or minced dried fruit	1 medium saucepan
	1 large spoon for mixing
½ cup honey	1 grinder, blender, or large knife for mincing
2 tbs. unsweetened prune juice	
1 tbs. lemon juice	measuring cup
1 tbs. orange juice	measuring spoons

---

1. Combine all ingredients in the saucepan.
2. Bring the mixture to a boil and turn the heat down immediately to low.
3. Simmer the mixture for 15 minutes, *stirring constantly.*
4. Remove from the stove and cool.

Whips

For additional ideas about fillings and icings, look at chapter 7. Whips make wonderful adornments for cakes.

16

Pies

A good pie can be one of the most mouth-watering treats of all—flaky crust, juicy filling, and a baking smell that brings people to the kitchen to bask in it.

You can buy a pie almost anywhere in any size and in any form. You can get tiny packaged one-person pies, boxed pies, frozen cooked pies, frozen uncooked pies, pie crust mixes, pie filling mixes, ready-made pie fillings in cans, and bakery pies. The one kind of pie that is hard to find is a genuine, home-baked, made from basic, fresh ingredients pie.

There is no pie that compares to a pie you make yourself —in flavor, smell, or texture. The reason for this is that when pies are mass produced in factories or even in the kitchens of most bakeries, quantity and not quality becomes the most important thing. Great amounts of sugar are used and, in the case of packaged pies, chemical preservatives are thrown in to insure lasting freshness on the shelves of stores.

If you've ever tasted a real home-baked pie fresh out of the oven with a flaky crust that melts in your mouth and a delicious filling that tastes like apples or peaches or custard instead of chemicals and gloppy, gooey filler, you'll understand. If you haven't tasted such a pie then you have a double treat in store for you: the satisfaction of making your own pie and the pleasure of eating it and serving it to others.

Pies are quite an old food with an interesting history. A pie is any meat, fish, fowl, fruit, or vegetable dish baked with a crust of pastry. Perhaps you've read about the famous Roman banquets that took place in the days of the Roman Empire. Well, in an effort to impress guests, hosts would serve elaborate concoctions including huge pies filled with live birds which would fly away when the top crust was cut open. In England, in the fourteenth century, meat and fish pies were common foods. In fact, meat pies are still popular in England today. By the sixteenth century, fruit pies were becoming popular and were given the name tarts. When English settlers came to the United States, they kept their taste for pies but had to adapt it to new foods and conditions in their new country. New pies such as pumpkin and cranberry were born.

With all of the world-wide immigration to the United States, pies gained new tastes, new textures, and an unending variety of possibilities. Try some of the recipes in this chapter and learn to bake an old and delicious food.

Basic Rules for Rolled Pastry Crusts

The crust is the most difficult part of any pie. However, if you follow these simple rules, your crusts should be flaky and delicious.

1. Use either unsalted butter or margarine in your pie crusts. Vegetable oils do not make for very light or flaky crusts.
2. While working with the pastry, handle it as little as possible. Too much prodding and squeezing will make it tough.
3. Make the pastry in a cool spot using *ice water* and *cold* butter or margarine.
4. Make sure your fingers are as cool as possible by dipping them in cold water.
5. *Never* knead pastry crust. Cut in the butter or margarine with two knives and then flake the dough *gently* with your cooled off fingertips until it is all mixed.
6. Before rolling out a pastry dough, place it in a refrigerator for ½ to 1 hour.
7. When rolling out pastry dough, *roll gently* on a lightly floured board, cold marble slab, or a clean formica counter top or table. (See directions for rolling out dough on p. 224, Basic Two-Crust Pie Dough.)

Never forget! A flaky crust depends upon gentle handling. The reason people often say that they can't bake a good pie is that they pound and squeeze the pastry.

Basic Two-Crust Pie Dough

Before you begin making any rolled pie crust, reread the rules for making a successful crust. Remember, the main rule is to handle the dough as little as possible, make the crust in a cool spot (a formica counter makes a more successful rolling surface than a wooden board), and always use ice water, cold butter or margarine, and keep your fingers cool.

INGREDIENTS	EQUIPMENT
2½ cups sifted whole-wheat pastry flour or unbleached flour	sifter or sieve
1 tsp. salt	1 large mixing bowl
¾ cup margarine or butter (1½ sticks)	rolling pin
3 to 4 tbs. ice water	waxed paper, tin foil, or cellophane wrap
	1 small sharp knife
	1 fork
	2 table knives for cutting in shortening
	pie tin (9-inch)
	measuring cup
	measuring spoons

1. Sift the presifted flour and the salt into the large bowl.
2. Make a hollow in the center of the flour and place the margarine or butter in it.
3. Cut in the butter or margarine with two knives.
4. With your fingertips, blend the flour and shortening (using a gentle pinching and rubbing motion) until the dough has a coarse, mealy consistency.
5. DON'T PRESS OR KNEAD THE DOUGH. FLAKE IT GENTLY.

6. When the dough is mealy, add about 3 or 4 tbs. of ice water and gently work the dough into a ball.
7. If you need a little more water, add it but the less water you use, the flakier your crust will be.
8. Pastry dough should stick together *but it should not* be doughy like bread dough.
9. Wrap your pastry ball in waxed paper, tin foil, or cellophane wrap, and put it in the refrigerator for at least 30 minutes.
10. ROLLING PASTRY DOUGH
    a. Divide the dough in half.
    b. Put ½ of the dough on a lightly floured surface.
    c. Dust your rolling pin with flour.
    d. Place the rolling pin in the center of the dough.
    e. Roll the rolling pin gently toward the edge of the dough.
    f. Keep rolling gently from the center of the dough to the edge, turning the dough around so that it gets shaped by the rolling into a circle.
    g. Keep rolling until the dough is large enough to fit the bottom and sides of your pie tin.
    h. Grease your pie tin.
    i. To lift up the dough, very gently roll the edge of the circle of pastry dough onto your rolling pin.
    j. Place it over the pie tin and put it gently into the tin.
    k. Trim off any excess dough around the edges with a knife.

Top Dough

    a. Roll out the pie dough in the same way as described above.
    b. After the pie is filled, place the crust on top of the filling.
    c. Press the edges of the top and bottom crusts to-

gether with your fingers or with a fork.
d. Trim off any excess dough with a sharp knife.
e. Using a fork, punch several holes in the top crust.
f. Bake according to the instructions in the filling recipe.

Sour Cream Pastry Dough

This is a delicate variation on the two-crust basic pie dough. This recipe must spend at least two hours in the refrigerator chilling, so leave plenty of time.

INGREDIENTS	EQUIPMENT
2 cups sifted unbleached flour	sifter or sieve
½ tsp. salt	1 large mixing bowl
1 cup (2 sticks) butter or margarine	rolling pin
6 tbs. sour cream	waxed paper, tin foil, or cellophane wrap
	1 small, sharp knife
	2 table knives for cutting in shortening
	1 fork
	pie tin (9-inch)
	measuring cup
	measuring spoons

1. Sift flour and salt into the mixing bowl.
2. Make a hollow in the center of the flour and place the margarine or butter in it.
3. Cut in margarine or butter with two knives.
4. With your fingertips, blend the flour and shortening to-

gether (see steps 3 and 4 in Basic Two-Crust Pie Dough recipe).

5. When the dough is mealy, gently, with your fingers, blend in the sour cream and form a ball of the dough.
6. Wrap the dough ball in waxed paper, tin foil, or cellophane wrap, and chill it in the refrigerator for at least 2 hours, preferably for a longer time.
7. Follow instructions for rolling out dough in Basic Two-Crust Pie Dough recipe.
8. Bake according to instructions in filling recipe.

Rolled Nut Pastry Crust

Making a pie crust with nuts is quite easy today because you can buy the nuts already ground. This recipe makes enough dough for a 9-inch two-crust pie. Give yourself enough time for the chilling of the dough if you decide to try it.

INGREDIENTS	EQUIPMENT
1¼ cups sifted whole-wheat pastry flour or unbleached flour	sifter or sieve
¾ cup finely ground nuts	1 large mixing bowl
½ cup butter or margarine (1 stick)	2 table knives
⅛ tsp. salt	rolling pin
4 tbs. ice water	tinfoil, waxed paper, or cellophane wrap
	1 9-inch pie pan
	measuring cup
	measuring spoons

1. Sift the presifted and measured flour and the salt into the large mixing bowl.
2. With your fingers, mix in the ground nuts.
3. Make a hollow in the center of the nut/flour mixture and place the butter or margarine in it.
4. Cut in the butter or margarine with two knives.
5. Gently work the cold butter or margarine into the flour/nut mixture with your fingertips (see steps 3 and 4 in Basic Two-Crust Pie Dough recipe).
6. When the dough resembles crumbly, coarse meal, add 1 tbs. of ice water and work it in.
7. Keep adding the ice water, one tablespoon at a time until you are able to form the dough into a ball. You may not need all of the ice water or you may need an extra tablespoon or two. Remember, the less water you use, the better.
8. Gently roll the dough into a ball, wrap it in tinfoil, waxed paper, or cellophane wrap, and chill it for about 2 hours.
9. After 2 hours, remove it from the refrigerator, divide it in half and roll it according to the instructions for the Basic Two-Crust Pie.
10. Grease your pie pan, carefully put the dough in it, fill it, cover with the top crust, and bake according to the instructions in your filling recipe.

Push Pastry Shell (No Rolling)

If you are in a hurry or are too timid to try a rolled pastry crust for your first pie, try making a push pastry crust. Push pastry crusts are meant for one-crust pies although you can easily cut a two-crust recipe in half and roll a dough for an open pie, too. Push pastry crusts are not as delicate as rolled crusts—they are thicker and a bit chewier—but they are, nevertheless, very good.

INGREDIENTS	EQUIPMENT
1½ cups sifted whole-wheat pastry flour or unbleached flour	sifter or sieve
	1 large mixing bowl
1½ tsp. honey	1 9-inch pie pan
1 tsp. salt	measuring cup
½ cup butter or margarine (cold)	measuring spoons
2 tbs. ice cold milk	2 table knives
	1 small dish
	1 fork

1. Sift the presifted flour and salt into the mixing bowl.
2. Make a hollow in the center of the flour mixture and place the butter or margarine in it.
3. Cut in the butter or margarine with two knives.
4. Gently work the butter or margarine into the flour with your fingertips until the mixture resembles coarse meal.
5. Mix the honey and the 2 tbs. of ice cold milk together in a small dish. Beat them with a fork so that they are thoroughly mixed together.
6. Pour the honey/milk mixture into the large bowl and work it into the dough with your fingertips. Do not knead the dough. This should be a gentle process and the flour should be dampened and flaky, not clotted together in a ball. This will make a softer dough than a rolled pastry dough.
7. When all ingredients are combined grease your pie pan.
8. Place the dough in the pie pan and gently press it evenly and firmly with your fingers so that it lines the pan.
9. Make sure that you press the dough up so that it covers the sides of the pan as well as the bottom. It should also partly cover the rim of the pan. Try to make it so that it has a uniform thickness.

10. You can press and pinch the edge of the dough to flute it.
11. If you are making an unbaked pie (one where the filling does not go into the oven, bake the pie crust for 12 to 15 minutes in a preheated 425° F. oven or until it is golden light brown.
12. Before putting the empty pie crust in the oven, prick the entire surface of it with a fork so that it won't buckle during baking.
13. For a baked pie, follow the baking instructions in the filling recipe.

Push Pie Pastry Made with Cereal or Nuts

Instead of flour, you can use dried cereal, ground nuts, or even poppy seeds to make a pie crust. It is suggested that you choose a plain cereal such as corn flakes or rice crispies, or a sweet, natural cereal such as granola. These crusts are all best for short-baking pies or no-baking pies since they are really precooked. Nut or cereal crusts are the easiest of all to make.

INGREDIENTS	EQUIPMENT
1½ cups crushed cornflakes, granola, ground nuts, or poppy seeds	1 large bowl for mixing
	1 large spoon for mixing
	1 9-inch pie pan
½ cup butter or margarine, softened	measuring cup
	measuring spoons
2 tbs. honey (for unsweetened nuts and cereal)	

---

1. In the large mixing bowl put all of the ingredients.
2. Mix and mash them together until all of the cereal, nuts,

or seeds are well coated with the shortening and honey.
3. Grease the pie pan.
4. Put all of the pastry dough into the pie pan and gently press it with your fingers until it covers the bottom, sides, and part of the rim of the pan. Try to make a uniform thickness.
5. For an unbaked pie, preheat the oven to 350° F.
6. Prick the surface with a fork and place the pie crust in the oven for 12 minutes.
7. Remove it from the oven, cool it down, and fill it.
8. For a baked pie, follow the directions in the filling recipe. Remember that this pie crust cannot really take a long baking time so only fill it with quick-baking fillings.

Coconut Pastry Crust

This is the easiest pastry crust of all. It must be used with unbaked pies but there are enough of those to make it a very useful recipe for you to know.

INGREDIENTS	EQUIPMENT
1½ cups unsweetened coconut, shredded	1 9-inch pie pan
2 tbs. butter or margarine, softened	

1. Preheat your oven to 300° F.
2. Spread (with your fingers) the 2 tablespoons of butter or margarine in the pie pan. Make sure that the entire bottom and sides are well coated with the shortening.
3. Firmly pat the 1½ cups of coconut shreds into the butter or margarine. Use all of the coconut.
4. Bake for 15 minutes in a 300° oven or until the coconut is lightly browned.

5. Cool and fill.
6. Fill this pie with fresh strawberries, blueberries, bananas, or sliced peaches or pears. See recipes in this section for open fruit pies. Top it off with a mound of whipped cream and you will have a perfect warm weather snack or dessert.

Any Berry Pie Filling

Choose your favorite berries—strawberries, blueberries, blackberries, raspberries—and try this pie. If you are baking it during the off season, use frozen but not canned berries. Commercially canned berries are usually packed in a heavy sugar syrup. Read the label on the frozen berries—many companies pack them without sugar. The best berry pie, of course, is made with fresh berries in season. Any berry pie can be served almost hot with ice cream or whipped cream heaped on top of each slice. Berry pie isn't half bad when served plain either.

INGREDIENTS	EQUIPMENT
1 2-crust pie pastry in 9-inch pan, uncooked	1 large mixing bowl
	1 large spoon for mixing
4 cups berries, washed, cleaned, and drained	measuring cup
	measuring spoons
¾ cup honey	cake rack
1 tbs. cornstarch	1 small knife
2 tsp. lemon juice	1 fork

1. Preheat oven to 425° F.
2. In the large mixing bowl, mix together the berries, honey, cornstarch, and lemon juice.

3. Spoon the mixture into the uncooked pie crust in the pie pan.
4. Cover the filling with the top crust. Trim off excess crust.
5. Seal the top and bottom edges of the pie crust together by pinching them with your fingers.
6. Either punch a few holes in the top crust with a fork or make a few small slits in the top crust with a knife. This allows steam to escape while the pie is cooking.
7. Bake at 425° for 45 minutes or until the crust is nicely browned.
8. Cool the pie on a cake rack.

Banana Pie

This is an ideal pie for a push pastry crust made of cereal, nuts, or coconut. Banana pie takes no time at all to make and its sweet goodness makes a wonderful dessert, snack, or party treat.

INGREDIENTS	EQUIPMENT
2 very ripe bananas	1 sieve
⅔ cup honey	1 heavy spoon
¼ tsp. salt	1 fork
¼ tsp. almond extract	egg beater or electric mixer
2 egg whites	1 large mixing bowl
1 9-inch pie crust, unbaked	1 large spoon for mixing
	1 medium mixing bowl
	cake rack
	measuring cup
	measuring spoons

1. Preheat oven to 350° F.
2. In the medium mixing bowl, mash the peeled bananas with a fork until they are quite soft.
3. Put the mashed bananas into the sieve and force them through the sieve with a heavy spoon back into the medium-sized bowl.
4. Put the honey, egg whites, salt, and almond extract into the large bowl.
5. Beat with the egg beater or electric mixer until the mixture is foamy and stands in peaks.
6. With the large spoon, gently fold the bananas into the egg/honey foam.
7. Put the mixture into an unbaked pie crust and place in oven.
8. Bake for 12 minutes at 350° or until slightly browned.
9. Cool on a rack and top with either whipped cream or the whipped cream-cheese frosting. Or serve plain.

Special Blueberry Pie

Since blueberry pie is my all-time favorite pie, I am including a separate recipe for it—above and beyond the Any Berry Pie recipe. This pie requires you to stick around the kitchen while it is baking because you must turn down the oven several times. However, it is worth it because the aroma of this pie cooking is almost as good as the taste of the pie when you're eating it. Serve it warm or cold, plain or topped with ice cream, whipped cream, or even sour cream. Any way you serve it, I think that you'll love it.

INGREDIENTS	EQUIPMENT
2-crust pastry, uncooked	1 small knife for trimming dough
3½ cups blueberries, washed, cleaned, and drained	sieve for rinsing blueberries
	pie pan

INGREDIENTS	EQUIPMENT
cinnamon	1 fork
1 tbs. butter or margarine	measuring cup
2 tsp. flour	measuring spoons
1 cup maple syrup (the pure kind) or honey	cake rack

1. Preheat oven to 450° F.
2. Prepare pastry crust and line the pie pan with ½ of the crust.
3. Fill the crust with the blueberries.
4. Sprinkle the blueberries with the flour and a little cinnamon.
5. Dot the blueberries with the butter or margarine. (Put tiny lumps of butter or margarine all over the top of the blueberries.)
6. Pour the maple syrup or honey evenly over the blueberries.
7. Place the top crust over the blueberries.
8. Trim off the excess dough.
9. Pinch together the top and bottom crusts around the edge of the pie with your fingers.
10. Cut a few slits in the top crust with your knife or fork.
11. Bake at 450° F. for 20 minutes. TURN DOWN THE OVEN TO 400° F. Bake at 400° F. for another 20 minutes. TURN DOWN THE OVEN TO 350° F. Bake for a final 20 minutes at 350° or until crust is nicely brown.
12. Cool pie on a cake rack.

Unbaked Fruit Pie

You can use almost any pie crust recipe for this pie. Just remember to bake the crust first if it needs baking. Use your favorite fruit for this pie or mix several kinds of fruit together if you wish. Serve this pie with whipped cream, ice cream, or grated nuts mixed with yoghurt on top of it.

INGREDIENTS	EQUIPMENT
3½ cups of your favorite fruit or berries, washed and cleaned	1 large mixing bowl
honey	1 large spoon for mixing
1 9-inch pie crust, cooked	1 large knife

1. If you are using half of the Basic Two-Crust Pie Dough recipe, the Sour Cream pastry recipe, the rolled nut, or push pastry shell, preheat your oven to 450° F. and bake the empty shell for 12 to 15 minutes or until it is golden brown. For other pastry recipes, follow the directions in the recipe.
2. Slice your fruit (pears, bananas, peaches, apples, apricots) into thin slices.
3. Put the fruit into the mixing bowl and stir in a little honey and taste. Keep adding honey until the fruit is sweet enough for you.
4. If you are using fresh berries, simply wash, clean, and drain them and put them in the bowl.
5. After your fruit is well mixed with the honey, spoon it into the *cooled* pie crust.
6. Top the fruit with whipped cream, yoghurt and nuts, or serve with ice cream.

Yoghurt and Cream Cheese Fruit Pie

You can use your favorite fruit yoghurt or plain yoghurt for this open-faced, uncooked pie. Choose either a cereal or nut push pastry shell or the coconut shell for this pie.

INGREDIENTS

1 9-inch pie crust, cooked

1 cup yoghurt, fruit or plain

2 8-oz. packages of cream cheese

1 tbs. honey (for fruit yoghurt) or
2 tbs. honey (for plain yoghurt)

½ tsp. vanilla extract (for plain yoghurt)

1½ cups sliced fresh fruit (bananas, peaches, pineapple, apricots) OR

1½ cups fresh whole berries

EQUIPMENT

1 heavy spoon for creaming

1 large mixing bowl

egg beater or electric mixer

1 large knife

1. Bake your pie crust according to the recipe and set aside.
2. In the mixing bowl, cream together the cream cheese, honey, and vanilla (if you are using plain yoghurt) .
3. Add the yoghurt and beat the mixture until it has the consistency of heavy whipped cream.
4. Spoon the mixture into the baked, cooled pie shell.
5. Arrange your sliced fruit or berries on the top of the pie.
6. Put it into the refrigerator and let it set (become a little solidified) . This should take approximately 1½ to 2 hours.
7. Serve cold.

Open-Faced Sour Cream Raisin Pie

This variation of a Pennsylvania Dutch recipe is a very easy pie to make. Use any pie crust recipe that can take a moderate amount of baking time but if you want completeness of flavor, try this pie with the Sour Cream Pastry Dough recipe. Use half of the recipe since this is an open pie.

INGREDIENTS	EQUIPMENT
1½ cups sour cream	1 large mixing bowl
1½ cups raisins	1 small dish for beaten eggs
1 cup honey	1 large spoon for mixing
2 eggs, slightly beaten	cake rack
1 tbs. flour	measuring cup
½ tsp. cinnamon	measuring spoons
½ tsp. nutmeg	
1 crust pastry, uncooked in pie pan	

1. Preheat oven to 350° F.
2. Put the honey, flour, nutmeg, and cinnamon in the large mixing bowl. Mix well.
3. Add the eggs and sour cream. Mix together very well.
4. Add the raisins and stir in very well.
5. Spoon the mixture into the unbaked pastry shell.
6. Bake for 35 minutes at 350° F.
7. Cool on a cake rack and then refrigerate until ready to serve.

Open Peach Pie

This is an unusual pie which requires that you take it out of the oven during baking to add additional ingredients. This open peach pie needs no additional adornments—it is a delicious treat all by itself.

INGREDIENTS	EQUIPMENT
1 9-inch pie crust, uncooked	1 large knife
1 tbs. melted butter	1 pastry brush
3 cups sliced fresh peaches	1 small mixing bowl
1 egg yolk	1 medium mixing bowl
¼ cup heavy cream	egg beater or electric mixer

INGREDIENTS

½ cup honey

½ tsp. cinnamon

EQUIPMENT

measuring cup

measuring spoons

cake rack

1. Preheat oven to 375° F.
2. Brush the pastry crust in the pan with the melted butter.
3. Arrange all of the peaches in the crust.
4. In the small mixing bowl, mix together the honey and the cinnamon.
5. Pour the honey and cinnamon over the peaches—distributing it as evenly as possible.
6. Put the pie in the oven and bake it for 20 minutes at 375°.
7. While the pie is baking, pour the heavy cream and the egg yolk into the medium mixing bowl. Beat this mixture until it is just beginning to get fluffy with the egg beater or electric mixer. *Do not beat it until it is whipped cream.*
8. When the pie has cooked for 20 minutes, remove it from the oven and pour the cream and egg mixture evenly over the peaches.
9. Return the pie to the oven and cook it for 15 minutes more or until the fruit is tender.
10. Cool on a rack and serve cool, not warm.

How to Cook a Fresh Pumpkin

There are a number of recipes in this book which use pumpkin. You can either buy cans of pumpkin (not pumpkin pie filling) or cook your own pumpkin from scratch. A side benefit of cooking your own pumpkin is that you also get a great many seeds which you can roast and eat. These, too, are delicious.

INGREDIENTS

1 whole pumpkin

EQUIPMENT

shallow baking pan large enough
   for pumpkin
1 sharp knife
1 large spoon
1 fork
2 large mixing bowls

1. Preheat oven to 350° F.
2. Cut the top out of your pumpkin. Leave the stem on for a handle. Set aside.
3. With the large spoon, scoop the seeds out of the pumpkin and put them into one of the mixing bowls.
4. Put the top back on the pumpkin and place the pumpkin in the shallow baking pan.
5. Bake in a 350° oven for 1½ hours or until the pumpkin is tender.
6. Remove the pumpkin from the oven and cool.
7. Peel the skin off the pumpkin (it will come off quite easily) and mash the pumpkin pulp with a fork. It is now ready to use.

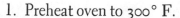

INGREDIENTS

1 whole pumpkin

EQUIPMENT

1 large, sharp knife

1 large, shallow baking pan

1 fork or food mill or sieve

1 large mixing bowl

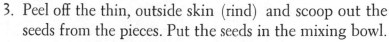

1. Preheat oven to 300° F.
2. Cut your pumpkin up into small strips or squares which are easy for you to handle.
3. Peel off the thin, outside skin (rind) and scoop out the seeds from the pieces. Put the seeds in the mixing bowl.
4. Put the pumpkin pieces in the baking pan and pour in about ¼ inch of water.
5. Bake at 300° F. for about 2½ hours or until each piece is tender.
6. Check the cooking pumpkin from time to time and add more water if it has evaporated.
7. When the pumpkin is done, either mash it with a fork (removing and discarding any stringy parts), put it through a food mill, or force it through a sieve.
8. It is now ready to use.

Pumpkin Seeds

Pumpkin seeds are sold in most markets in the nut section. It would therefore be a shame to simply throw away your seeds. As a matter of fact, even if you are simply using a pumpkin as a Jack-O-Lantern, save the seeds and do the following:

Pies

INGREDIENTS	EQUIPMENT
raw pumpkin seeds	1 sieve
	paper towels
	1 cookie sheet or large baking pan
	1 jar for storage

1. Preheat the oven to 350° F.
2. Put your pumpkin seeds in the sieve and hold it under cold water until much of the pulp which is sticking to them is loosened.
3. Shake the sieve a few times to drain out any excess water.
4. Set the sieve down and, with your hands, begin moving the seeds from the sieve to the paper towels. Try to discard the loose pulp as you do this.
5. After all of the seeds are on the paper towels, pat them dry with a clean paper towel.
6. Place the dry seeds on a cookie sheet or large baking pan, ungreased.
7. Before putting them in the oven, spread the seeds evenly over the pan and try to pick out any remaining pulp.
8. Bake for 15 minutes in a 350° oven or until the seeds are light brown.
9. If you wish, you can sprinkle the seeds with salt before you put them in a jar for future eating pleasure.
10. Do not put the lid on the jar until the seeds are cool.

Pumpkin Pie Filling

Pumpkin pie is especially good in the fall or winter because it seems to give one a warm glow of satisfaction after eating it. Late fall is, of course, the time of year when whole, fresh pumpkins are available but you can, with the help of the canning industry, make spicy pumpkin pie year-round if you wish.

INGREDIENTS

1 unbaked pie shell in a pie pan (use the push pastry recipe or ½ of the Basic Two-Crust Pie Dough)

½ cup honey

1¾ cups cooked, mashed pumpkin or canned pumpkin*

¾ cup milk or condensed milk

¼ cup molasses

2 eggs, well beaten (until light and foamy)

1 tsp. cinnamon

½ tsp. nutmeg

½ tsp. ground ginger

½ tsp. salt

EQUIPMENT

1 large mixing bowl

1 small mixing bowl for beating eggs

1 large spoon for mixing

measuring cup

measuring spoons

1 table knife

1 fork for beating eggs

cake rack

1. Preheat oven to 450° F.
2. In the large mixing bowl, blend together the pumpkin, honey, molasses, cinnamon, nutmeg, ginger, and salt.
3. Add the milk and beaten eggs. Mix in thoroughly.
4. Pour the mixture into the unbaked pie shell.
5. Bake at 450° for 10 minutes. TURN DOWN HEAT to 350° F. and bake for 45 additional minutes or until done.
6. Test for doneness. Take a clean, dry table knife and stick it into the center of the pie. If the knife comes out

* Be sure to buy canned pumpkin and not canned pumpkin pie mix if you are not using fresh pumpkin.

clean, the pie is done. If it comes out with some of the filling sticking to it, it needs some more time.

7. Cool on a cake rack.

Pumpkin pie is great plain or served with whipped cream on top.

Old-Fashioned Apple Pie

No packaged or frozen apple pie compares to one you make yourself. Served warm with ice cream, cheddar cheese, or plain, it is a mouth-watering treat that can't be duplicated in a commercial kitchen.

INGREDIENTS	EQUIPMENT
pastry for a 2-crust pie, uncooked	1 9-inch pie pan
9 to 10 peeled and thinly sliced medium-sized apples	1 large mixing bowl
	1 large spoon for mixing
½ cup honey	1 small knife
1 tsp. cinnamon	1 large knife for slicing
2 tbs. butter or margarine	cake rack
	measuring cup
	measuring spoons

1. Preheat oven to 425° F.
2. Grease the pie pan and line it with half of the pastry crust.
3. In the large mixing bowl, mix together the apple slices, honey, and cinnamon.
4. Place a layer of the honeyed apples in the pie pan.
5. Dot the layer of apples with some of the butter or margarine.
6. Repeat steps 4 and 5 until you have used up all of the apples and butter. The pie pan should be *heaped* with apples, not level.
7. Roll out the top crust and place it on top of the pie.

You will have to roll this top crust a bit larger than you would for other pies to cover the heaped apples.

8. Trim off the excess dough with the small knife.
9. Seal the edges of the top and bottom crusts together by pinching them with your fingers.
10. Make two or three slits in the top crust with your small knife.
11. Bake for 45 minutes at 425° F. or until the crust is a nice golden brown.
12. Cool on a cake rack.

Sweet Potato Pie

Sweet potato pie is an old American pie with strong roots in the black and southern communities of the United States. It is a delicious, spicy dessert which should be tried once by any skeptic who feels that sweet potatoes should only be eaten as a side dish to turkey.

INGREDIENTS	EQUIPMENT
1½ cans (1 lb. cans) sweet potatoes or yams, drained	1 large mixing bowl
	sieve for draining potatoes
1 large can of evaporated milk (14½ oz. can)	pie tin (9-inch)
	egg beater or electric mixer
½ cup honey	fork
2 eggs, slightly beaten	1 large spoon for mixing
½ tsp. salt	measuring spoons
¼ tsp. ginger	measuring cup
1 tsp. cinnamon	1 table knife
½ tsp. allspice	1 small, sharp knife
¼ tsp. nutmeg	
pastry for 1-crust pie, uncooked	

1. Preheat oven to 350° F.
2. In the sieve, drain the sweet potatoes or yams over the sink.
3. Put the drained sweet potatoes or yams in the large mixing bowl.
4. Mash them with a fork until they are smooth.
5. With the egg beater or electric mixer, beat the potatoes or yams until they are very well mashed.
6. Add the milk and the eggs to the potatoes. Beat for about a minute.
7. Add the honey, salt, ginger, cinnamon, allspice, and nutmeg. Mix in well with the large spoon.
8. Line your greased pie pan with the pastry crust and trim off any excess crust around the edge of the pan.
9. Pour the sweet potato mixture into the unbaked pie shell.
10. Bake for approximately 45 minutes at 350° or until done.
11. Test for doneness: Push the tip of a clean, dry table knife into the center of the pie. If it comes out clean, it is done.
12. Cool on a cake rack.

Peach or Apple Custard Pie

This recipe combines the smoothness of a custard pie with the sweetness of a fruit pie. The only trick to making this pie is getting it into the oven without spilling the custard. Follow the directions carefully, however, and you'll have that problem solved.

INGREDIENTS	EQUIPMENT
pastry for 1-crust pie, uncooked	1 medium saucepan
2 cups milk, scalded (see Chap. 2)	1 9-inch pie pan

INGREDIENTS

4 eggs, well beaten
1 cup thinly sliced apples or peaches
½ cup honey
½ tsp. cinnamon
¼ tsp. nutmeg
¼ tsp. salt
1 tsp. vanilla

EQUIPMENT

1 fork
pastry brush
1 large knife for slicing
1 small knife
1 large spoon for mixing
1 large mixing bowl
cake rack
measuring cup
measuring spoons
1 medium mixing bowl for beaten eggs

1. Preheat oven to 400° F.
2. Put your pie crust in a greased pie pan and prick the sides and bottom of the crust with a fork. Trim off excess crust.
3. Brush some of the beaten egg on the uncooked crust.
4. Bake the crust in the oven for 5 minutes. Remove it and set it aside.
5. Turn down the oven to 350° F.
6. Arrange the peach or apple slices on the bottom of the pie pan, using all of the fruit.
7. In the large mixing bowl, mix together the honey, cinnamon, and nutmeg.
8. Brush 1 tablespoon of this mixture on the peaches or apples.
9. In the large mixing bowl, combine the remaining eggs, honey, salt, and vanilla. Mix well.
10. Add the scalded milk to the egg/honey mixture very slowly and stir very well.
11. Gently pour all but 1 cup of the milk/egg/honey mix-

ture into the pie pan. The apples or peaches will float to the top.

12. Pull the shelf of your oven out slightly and set the filled pie pan on it.

13. Pour the rest of the milk/egg/honey mixture into the pie pan and gently push the shelf back into place.

14. Bake this pie for 30 to 35 minutes at 350° F. or until done.

15. Test for doneness: Stick the tip of a dry, clean knife into the center of the pie. If it comes out clean, it is done.

16. Cool on a cake rack. This pie is best served cool or cold.

Suggested Books

There are so many cookbooks available that is difficult to recommend only a few. The following list includes some of my favorite cookbooks and food reference books. All of the cookbooks in the list are clearly written and easy to follow even when the recipes involved are quite elegant.

Beck, Bodog F., M.D. and Smedley, Doree, *Honey and Your Health*. New York: Bantam Books, 1971.

This is a reprint of an old book. It is filled with interesting information about the history, traditions, superstitions, and uses of honey. It also contains a few really fine recipes and makes an excellent paperback reference book for your library.

Beard, James, *The James Beard Cookbook*. New York: Dell Publishing Co., 1966.

This is one of the best all-purpose cookbooks around. Mr. Beard gives clear, easy-to-follow directions for recipes which range from simple, hearty foods to gourmet delights. This is not a health food cookbook but Mr.

Beard advocates the use of fresh, unprocessed produce and you can substitute honey for the sugar in the recipes if you wish.

Brown, Edith and Sam, *Cooking Creatively with Natural Foods*. New York: Ballantine Books, 1973.
This book includes a good section describing natural foods and specialized products you will find in health food and natural food stores. It also has over 400 recipes including juices, soups, salads, main dishes, breads, and sweets. When I use this book, I substitute honey for the raw sugar used in some of the recipes.

Elkon, Juliette, *The Honey Cookbook*. New York: Paperback Library, 1972.
In addition to a good, clear explanation of how honey is produced, this book contains many good recipes for main courses as well as all kinds of desserts.

Hewitt, Jean, *The New York Times Natural Foods Cookbook*. New York: Avon Books, 1972.
In addition to being attractive, this cookbook has a very wide choice of recipes for all occasions which are presented in an easy step-by-step fashion. Access to a health or natural food store is helpful if you use this book because many of the ingredients necessary are not available in supermarkets.

Rainey, Jean, *How to Shop for Food*. Barnes & Noble, 1972. New York: If you want to find out how to judge food products, find real bargains, read labels, understand U.S. government inspection marks, learn how to store food, and gain further information about food additives and nutrition, this ninety-five-cent book (sold in many supermarkets for less) is a wonderful resource.

Stoner, Carol, ed. *Stocking up: How to Preserve Foods You Grow Naturally*. Emmaus, Pa.: Rodale Press, 1973.

You don't have to grow your own food to use this book. Learn how to make your own cottage cheese, butter, and fruit butters. Learn how to cook with all kinds of nuts and seeds, how to preserve and pickle fruits and vegetables, and how to freeze and can food. The clear writing and useful photographs in this book make it an excellent guide for a novice cook.

U.S. Department of Agriculture, *Composition of Foods, Agricultural Handbook No. 8*. Washington, D.C.: Government Printing Office, 1963.
If you are at all curious about the nutritional value of just about any food you can think of, this book is perfect for you. Parts of the handbook are really too technical for most people but the pages and pages of charts are both useful and easy to read.

Vaughan, Beatrice, *Real, Old Time Yankee Maple Cookery*. Brattleboro, Vt.: Stephen Greene Press, 1969.
This small, very pretty paperback has a wealth of easy-to-follow, mouth-watering recipes which make good use of pure maple syrup. Meats, vegetables, puddings, cakes, breads, and pies all benefit from the unique New England maple touch. The Stephen Greene Press also publishes a number of other books which offer old American recipes.

Index

Beverages (*Cont.*)
    orange drink for a crowd, 47
    orange milk drink, 46–47
Biscuits, 161–63
    basic, 161
    cheese, 163
    raisin-nut, 163
    round, 163
    square, 162
Biscuit cutter, 37
Blanched, 29
Blend, 29
Boil, 29
Bowls, mixing, 38
Bread, 132–54
    history, 132–35
    equipment, 141
    kneading, 135–36
    rising, 137–40
    test for doneness, 140–41
Bread board, 37
Breads, 142–58, 166–67
    apple, 146
    banana with yoghurt, 152–53
    Boston brown, 147–49
    chapattis, 166–67
    cinnamon nut, 145–46
    fruit and nut, 153–54
    hom yoke bow, 156–58
    lemon and molasses, 149–50
    peanut butter, 146–47
    pumpkin, 154–55
    raisin, 143–44
    rice, 150–51
    rye nut, 142–43
    three easy, 144–46
Broil, 30
Brown, 30
Brush, 30
B vitamins, 8–9

C
Cake rack, 37
Cakes, 186–99; baking time, 130; cooling, 131; history, 184–85; removing from tin, 131; test for doneness, 130
    carrot layer, 192–93
    chestnut cakes, 198–99
    fruit cake, 188–89
    old-fashioned gingerbread, 186–87
    orange, 189–91
    peanut butter, 191–92
    pumpkin layer, 196–97
    quick carob, 197–98
    raisin loaf, 187–88
    sponge roll, 194–95
Calcium, 6
Calories, 19
Candies, 65–78; history, 65–66
    Cracker Jacks, 79–80
    easy peanut butter, 69–70
    fruit bars, 76–77
    halvah, 74–75
    honey drop, 67–68
    honey marshmallows, 77–78
    marzipan, 68–69
    mixed fruit balls, 73–74
    no-cook fudge, 71–72
    peanut butter, 70–71
Carbohydrates, 4
Carob, 19
Cellophane wrap, 30
Chocolate, 18
Chop, 3
Cobalamin, 9
Concentrates, 41
Cookie cutter, 37
Cookie sheet, 38
Cookies, 184–85, 200–12; cooling, 131; test for doneness, 131
    almond, 200–201
    almond macaroons, 203–204

Cookies (*Cont.*)
   carob, 204–205
   coconut, 205–206
   fortune, 201–203
   fruit pinwheel, 209–12
   no-flour nut, 207
   spice, 208–209
Cooking terms, 29–33
Cooling baked products, 131
Core, 30
Corn flour, 122
Corn meal, 122
Crackers, 163–66
   basic, 163–64
   sesame seed, 164–66
Creaming, 30
Cube, 30
Cupcakes, 168–77; cooling, 169; removing, 170; test for doneness, 169; using cake recipes, 169
   banana, 176–77
   carob, 173–74
   fruit, 172–73
   peanut butter raisin, 174–76
   regular old cupcakes, 170–71
Custard cups, 82
Custards, 83–87, 246–48; history, 82
   plain egg, 83–84
   fruit, 85–87
   orange, 84–85
   pie, 246–48
Cut-in, 30
Cutter, cookie and biscuit, 37

D
Dash, 30
Dice, 30
Dieters, 19–21
Dips. *See* Party snacks
Dishes, bowls, cups, 38

Doneness
   bread, 140–41
   cakes, 130
   cookies, 130–31
   cupcakes, 169
   muffins, 169
Dot, 30
Double boiler, 39
Doubling recipes, 129
Drinks. *See* Beverages
Dust, 31; directions, 128
D, vitamin, 10

E
Egg beater, 36
Egg separating, 32
Egg temperature, 129
Electric mixer, 35
Equivalents, 27–39
E, vitamin, 10

F
Fat, body, 19–20
Fats, 4–6; cholesterol, 5–6, 124; oily skin, 5; saturated, 5, 124; unsaturated, 5, 124
Fillings, 219–20
   dried fruit, 220
   raisin, 219
Flour, description, 119; 118–23 sifting, 122
   bleached, 120
   corn, 122
   enriched, 120
   gluten, 121, 137
   soy, 122
   stone ground, 122
   unbleached, 120
   wheat germ, 121
   white, 119–20

Flour (*Cont.*)
    whole grain, 123
    whole wheat, 120–21
    whole wheat pastry, 121
    rye, 121–22
Frostings, 213–20
    banana, 218–19
    cream cheese, 215–16
    honey, 216–17
    no-cook carob, 214–15
    raisin coconut, 217–18
    whipped cream, 214
    whips, 220
Fruit, canned, 99; dried, 100; frozen, 99–100
Fruit concoctions, 98–108
    apple butter, 104–105
    applesauce, 104–105
    baked or broiled bananas, 108
    baked pears or apples, 105–106
    broiled grapefruit, 107
    dried fruit in apple juice, 101–102
    fruit compote, 100–101
    fruit and honey, 104
    fruit and special sour cream, 102–103
    poached cherries, 103
Fruit drink, 41
Fruit juice drink, 41

G

Garnish, 31
Gluten, 137
Gluten flour, 121
Grate, 31
Grater, 38
Grease, 31
Greasing pans, 128
Grill, 31
Grind, 31

H

Halving recipes, 129
Healthful foods, 1–21
Honey, 17–18

I

Ice, 31
Icings. *See* Frostings
Iodine, 7
Iron, 7

J

Juice, 41

K

Knead, 31
Kneading, directions, 135–36
Knives, 35
K, vitamin, 10

L

Labels, reading, 13–14

M

Magnesium, 7
Margarine, 124, 128
Measurements, 22–29, 128
Measuring cups, 24–25, 38
Measuring, 23–26
    butter and margarine, 25–26
    dry ingredients, 25
    liquids, 25
Measuring spoons, 23
Mince, 31
Minerals, 6–7
Mixing bowls, 38
Molasses, 15–16
Mortar and pestle, 36
Muffins, 168–70, 177–83; cooling, 169; removing from tin, 170; test for doneness, 169

Muffins (*Cont.*)
  applesauce, 177–78
  blueberry, 180–81
  corn, 179
  scones, 181–82
  yoghurt raisin nut, 182–83
Muffin tin, 39

N
Nectar, 41
Niacin, 8–9
Nutrients, 2–10
Nutrition, 2

O
Oil, to, 31
Oiling pans, 128
Oils, 123–25
  cold pressed, 125
  nut, 124–25
  olive, 125
  vegetable, 124–25
Oils, uses, 123
Orange juice products, 42
Ounces, liquid, 26–27; weight, 26–27
Oven, differences, 127–40; placement, 129–30; temperature, 127, 129, 140; thermometer, 37, 127

P
Pan broil, 31
Pare, 31
Party Snacks, 51–64
  candy apples, 58–59
  cream cheese dips, 57
  deviled eggs, 55–56
  fruit treats, 58
  guacamole, 60
  Mrs. DePalma's pizza, 52–55
  noodle kugel, 61–62

Party Snacks (*Cont.*)
  potato kugel, 63–64
  roasted almonds, 56–57
  salmon dip, 61
  spicy cheese dip, 59–60
Pastry brush, 36
Pestle, mortar and, 36
Phosphorus, 7
Pie crusts, 222–32; directions, 224–26; rules, 222–23
  basic two-crust dough, 223–26
  coconut pastry, 231–32
  push pastry, cereal or nuts, 230–31
  push pastry, no rolling, 228–30
  rolled nut, 227–28
  sour cream, 226–27
Pie fillings, 232–46
  any berry, 232–33
  apple or peach custard, 246–47
  banana, 233–34
  open peach, 238–39
  old-fashioned apple, 244–45
  pumpkin, 242–44
  sour cream raisin, 237–38
  special blueberry, 234–35
  sweet potato, 245–46
  unbaked fruit, 235–36
  yoghurt and cream cheese fruit, 236–37
Pies, 221–46; basic rules, 222–23; history, 222
Pinch, 32
Potato masher, 36
Pots and pans, 38
Preheating, 127
Premeasuring, 128–29
Protein foods, 3
Proteins, 3–4; complete, 3; incomplete, 4
Puddings, 87–92; history, 81
  baked fruit, 88–89
  bread, 91–92

Index